W9-APL-976

Adorable Felted Animals

30 EASY & INCREDIBLY LIFELIKE NEEDLE FELTED PALS

Gakken

Handmade Series

TUTTLE Publishing

Tokyo │Rutland, Vermont│ Singapore

Dogs

Dick

Taro

Liz

John

dog (dôg, dŏg) n. **1.** A domesticated carnivorous mammal, *Canis familiaris*, raised in a wide variety of breeds and held to have orig. derived from several wild species. **2.** Any of various animals of the family Cani-

Boss

TECHN

Papir

hamster
five-piglets

Contents

The creations in this book are made from Hamanaka wool felt, a popular Japanese brand, and using Hamanaka felting needles and other materials. There are many brands of wool and tools available through your local shops and online. In certain areas, the wool in local shops may be locally supplied.

The Japanese Shiba

Pricked-up ears and a curled tail are the signature of the Shiba, one of the most popular of the Japanese dog breeds. The gaze of those adorable eyes really stirs the heart, and the paws in their white "socks" are seriously cute.

DESIGN: Sareee   **HOW TO MAKE IT:** p34   ❀ **HEIGHT:** 3⅛ in (8cm)

The Hokkaido Dog

The Hokkaido Dog stands the cold well and is a very patient breed. Extremely intelligent, it is also used as a hunting dog. The pose with the slightly tilted head is charming.

DESIGN: Sareee **HOW TO MAKE IT:** p35 ❧ **HEIGHT:** 3½ in (9cm)

Miniature Dachshund (Left)

With its characteristic long body and short legs, the Miniature Dachshund is one of the most popularly ranked breeds.

DESIGN: Sareee **HOW TO MAKE IT:** p36–37 🐾 **LENGTH:** 6¼ in (16cm)

The Chihuahua (Right)

Huge, moist eyes and a little body give the Chihuahua its charm. Its black and white coat and facial markings that resemble eyebrows give it an air of dignity.

DESIGN: Sareee **HOW TO MAKE IT:** p38–39 🐾 **HEIGHT:** 4 in (10cm)

Rabbits

With its large ears and little, round tail, the rabbit is a popular pet, even taking other small animals into account. Standing up on its hind legs and looking up, its pose is adorable.

DESIGN: Satomi Fujita   **HOW TO MAKE IT:** p40–41
HEIGHT: Standing figure—4⅜ in (11cm)   **LENGTH:** Prone figure—2¾ in (7cm)

Golden Retriever

These two dogs snuggled together look just like the real thing.
The look of the mother dog gazing at her pup warms the heart.

DESIGN: Sareee **HOW TO MAKE IT:** p42–44

🐾 **HEIGHT:** Parent dog—4½ in (11.5cm) **LENGTH:** Puppy—6¼ in (16cm)

*Detailed instructions for making the puppy on this page are given on page 28 in the "Basics of Needle Felting" section. Make the puppy's tail thin and smooth and the mother's full and fluffy.

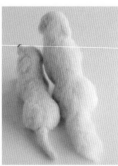

li kväll. De tog varann i handen
måsen som satt på sin påle och
nnen.

Labrador Retriever

The Labrador's mild temperament and friendly nature allow it to work as a guide dog or security dog. It looks similar to the Golden Retriever but its coat is shorter.

DESIGN: Sareee   **HOW TO MAKE:** p45   🐾 **HEIGHT:** 4⅜ in (11cm)

Toy Poodle (1)

This small dog is one of the best known of the lap dogs. Its curly coat gives it a cuteness just like that of a soft teddy bear. The pink ear decorations add to the charm.

DESIGN: Satomi Fujita   **HOW TO MAKE IT:** p46
❧ **HEIGHT:** 2⅛ in (5.5cm)

The Pomeranian (2)

Much loved by Queen Victoria, the Pomeranian has long, fluffy fur. Its happy frolicking nature gives it a prettiness you want to reach out and pat. With its head to one side, it has a playful look.

DESIGN: Satomi Fujita   **HOW TO MAKE IT:** p47
❧ **HEIGHT:** 2 in (5cm)

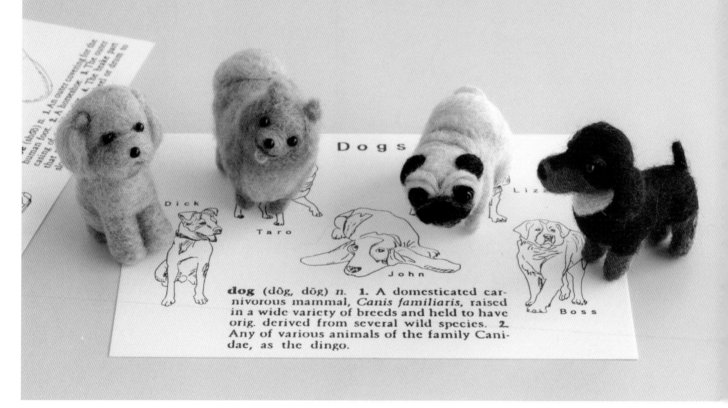

The Pug (3)

A little body and big, slightly bulging eyes; a wrinkly face and squashed-in nose—the Pug has so many loveable features. At first glance, it looks like a bulldog, but its whole body is more compact.

DESIGN: Satomi Fujita   **HOW TO MAKE IT:** p48
❧ **HEIGHT:** 1¼ in (3 cm)

The Dachshund (4)

A long body, short legs, long face and big, floppy ears characterise this breed. With a very cheerful disposition, its little mannerisms are amusing and mischievous. The blue scarf tied around its neck is nice touch.

DESIGN: Satomi Fujita   **HOW TO MAKE IT:** p49
❧ **HEIGHT:** 2⅛ in (5.5cm)

Shih Tzu

Shaggy hair is characteristic of this friendly breed whose hardy ancestors lived on the plateaus of Tibet. Perhaps because it was a favorite of noble-women, it seems somehow to come across as a bit prim.

DESIGN: Satomi Fujita   **HOW TO MAKE IT:** p50   ❧ **HEIGHT:** 3⅛ in (8cm)

| Toy Poodle | The Pomeranian | The Pug | The Dachshund |

Welsh Terrier (Airedale)

Contrasting black and tan markings that give it the look of wearing clothes are the trademark of this breed. Its long, slim legs and short upright tail are attractive features.

DESIGN: Satomi Fujita   **HOW TO MAKE IT:** p51   ♣ **HEIGHT:** 4 in (10cm)

Siamese Cat

A narrow face and a color pointed coat are characteristics of the Siamese Cat, a shorthair breed from Thailand. Its long, thin tail and blue eyes that you could drown in create a cool impression.

DESIGN: Campanella **HOW TO MAKE IT:** p52 ♣ **HEIGHT:** 4 in (10cm)

The American Tabby

With its big, erect ears, rounded face and sharp gaze, this is the archetypical cat. The beautiful swirling markings running along its back and down to its tail are charming.

DESIGN: Campanella　**HOW TO MAKE IT:** p53–55　🐾 **HEIGHT:** 4¼ in (10.5cm)

Chinchilla Silver Cat (Left)

Related to the Persian cat, the Chinchilla Silver Cat is a long-haired breed, as is the Norwegian Forest Cat. This figure's cute appeal comes from its pose—standing on its hind legs as if it's about to roll the ball.

Norwegian Forest Cat (Right)

This cat is said to have lived in the forests of Norway and stands the cold well. Its silhouette veiled in a luxurious coat gives it a gorgeous appearance.

DESIGN: Campanella   **HOW TO MAKE IT:** (left) p56–57 (right) p58–59   ❧ **HEIGHT:** (left) 3⅜ in [8.5cm] (right) 4 in [10cm]

The Abyssinian

The Abyssinian has a slim, sleek body, large ears and well defined almond-shaped eyes. The dark marking running from its head down the length of its spine is a characteristic of the breed.

DESIGN: Campanella   **HOW TO MAKE IT:** p60–61   ❀ **HEIGHT:** 4⅜ in (11cm)

The Munchkin

Just like the Dachshund, the munchkin is defined by its long body and short limbs. Its adorable gait on those short legs is behind its rapid rise in popularity.

DESIGN: Campanella   **HOW TO MAKE IT:** p62   ❦ **HEIGHT:** 3⅜ in (8.5cm)

Little Birds

Here's a bunch of little birds with beautiful colorful feathers.
The Budgerigar and the Cockatiel can be made in two sizes.

The Budgerigar (Left)   **The Java Finch** (Center)   **The Cockatiel** (Right)

DESIGN: Satomi Fujita   **HOW TO MAKE IT:** p63–65   ↓ **LENGTH:** (left) 2 in [5cm] (right) 1¾ in [4.5cm]

The Budgerigar (Left) The Cockatiel (Right)

DESIGN: Satomi Fujita   **HOW TO MAKE IT:** p63–65   ↓ **LENGTH:** (left) 2¾ in [7cm] (right) 3 in [7.5cm]

Chipmunks

The chipmunk has a clear band of black running down its back and a long tail. Maybe the way it uses its little front paws to eat is the secret to its popularity?

DESIGN: Satomi Fujita   **HOW TO MAKE IT:** (large) p66 (small) p67   ❧ **LENGTH:** (large) 3½ in [9cm] (small) 1¼ in [3cm]

AS KLETTERBÜBLEIN

ER WIENER WERKSTÄTTE BILDERBOGEN Nº

Tiny Birds

At only about ⅞ in (2cm) tall, these three different birds are miniature size. These cute birds can be made with only a little bit of left over felt.

Red-breasted Parakeet (Left)   White Java Finch (Center)
Peach-faced Lovebird (Right)

DESIGN: Satomi Fujita   **HOW TO MAKE IT:** p68–69   ↓ **LENGTH:** (left) 1 in [2.5cm] (center) ¾ in [1.8cm] (right) ⅞ in [2.2cm]

Ferrets

With its markings that resemble an eye mask, the ferret is a member of the weasel family.
Its peach-colored nose and tightly drawn-in mouth are heartwarming.

(large) **DESIGN:** Campanella   **HOW TO MAKE IT:** p70   ❀ **HEIGHT:** 6 in (15cm)
(small) **DESIGN:** Satomi Fujita   **HOW TO MAKE:** p71   ❀ **HEIGHT:** 2 in (5cm)

Hamsters

These hamster siblings have chubby, round bodies. Is the way they stuff their cheeks full of their favorite sunflower seeds similar to human children's behavior?

DESIGN: Satomi Fujita   **HOW TO MAKE IT:** p72–73 (standing figure)
HEIGHT: Standing figure—2½ in (6.5cm)   ♛ **LENGTH:** Prone figure—2½ in (6.5cm)

Three Kinds of Rabbit

From boxes appliqued with flowers, rabbits poke out their heads just a little to peek around.
You can change their look simply by slightly altering the color combinations.

DESIGN: s@chi   **HOW TO MAKE IT:** p74–75   ❦ **HEIGHT:** 3 in (7.5cm)

Phone Strap Decorations

Wouldn't it be nice to have your pet with you all the time? Attach strap clasps to these felt pet figures and hang them from your cell phone or purse.

Miniature Shiba (1) Miniature Hokkaido Dog (2)

DESIGN: Satomi Fujita **HOW TO MAKE IT:** (Miniature Shiba) p76 (Miniature Hokkaido Dog) p77

Miniature Schnauzer (3) Miniature Dachshund (4)

DESIGN: Sareee **HOW TO MAKE IT:** p78–79 ❀ **HEIGHT:** (from left) 1¾, 2, 3, 3 in (4.5, 5, 7.5, 7.5cm)

The Basics of Needle Felting 🐾

Before you start

"Needle felting" is a form of craft in which a special needle is used to create shapes from wool.
When the fluffy wool is poked repeatedly with this needle, the fibers mat together
to transform into felt. The degree of firmness created is up to you—the more the needle is
worked in and out of the wool, the firmer the figure becomes, while reducing the number of times
you poke the wool will result in a fluffier, softer figure. The tip of the needle is sharp,
so take care not to accidentally prick your finger when working.
In this book, a technique known as "implanting" has been used to create extremely life
like markings on the coats of some of the animals such as dogs and cats.
Take a good look at the coat of the animal you are recreating in felt
and have a go at the implanting technique.

Materials and Tools 🐾

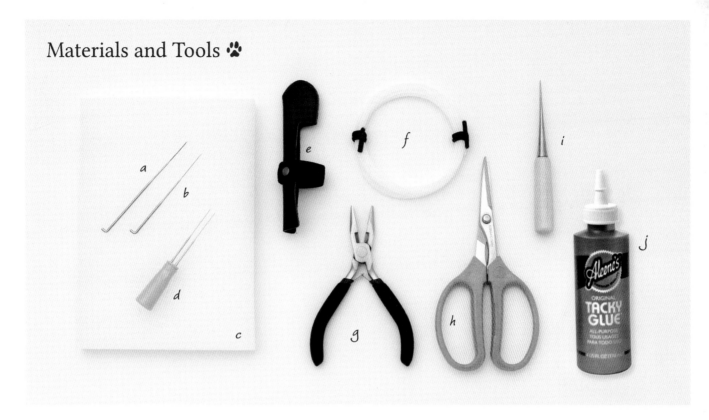

a **FELTING NEEDLES** These special needles have several small barbs at the tip. When poking through the wool, the barbs catch the fibers and mat them together, creating the felt.

b **EXTRA-FINE FELTING NEEDLES** This needle is finer than [a] and is suitable for intricate work.

c **A FELTING MAT** This is a mat especially for felting. It makes working with the needle easier and is helpful to prevent it from going in all directions.

d **A FELTING NEEDLE HOLDER** This holder holds two needles. Working with two needles at once allows you to felt faster, so this is a very convenient tool. This type contains needles that can be replaced if they get bent.

e **A FINGER COVER FOR NEEDLE FELTING** This cover protects your finger from getting pricked while working.

f **A FLORIST WIRE** This is inserted into the base of limbs when creating figures in active poses to help keep them in shape.

g **PLIERS** Used for bending florist wire.

h **SCISSORS** Craft scissors that cut well.

i **AN AWL** Used for creating holes for eyes. For small eyes, the tip of a needle can also be used to create holes.

j **CRAFT GLUE** Fast-drying craft adhesive that turns transparent when dry.

FELTING WOOL (ROVING) Created using a special manufacturing method, this wool is the most suitable quality for felting. It is available in types including natural, mix, solid and tweed, with an assortment of blending methods and colors on the market. The solid type shown in the photo is a standard type made from 100% merino wool which comes in many colors.

WOOL BATTING This is wool that has been worked into a kind of floss. It is suited for use as a base when needle felting, as it forms into neat shapes when punched lightly with a needle.

SOLID EYES This can be used to create animals' eyes and noses. Apply adhesive to the long shank and insert it firmly into the figure.

❧ A Step-by-step Lesson with Sareee

On these pages, the steps involved in making the Golden Retriever puppy on page 8 are explained, from how to create the base to the implanting technique that completes the figure, as a general example for all projects. For materials needed, a full-size diagram of the face and the order in which to complete steps, please refer to pages 42–44. The order in which to create parts and how to give the figure expression differ from project to project, so refer to the photos at the start of the book and follow the order of steps given on each page.

A Create base for body and front legs using florist wire ❧

1 Cut florist wire to 4 in (10cm) for the body and 5¾ in (14.5cm) for the front leg section.

2 Using pliers, curve back each end of the florist wire for the legs.

3 Flatten the florist wire using the end of the pliers.

4 Bend in half and find the center.

5 Wind the florist wire for the body section around the piece for the legs.

6 Form the wire into the shape of the letter T.

B Create the base for each part, referring to the full-size diagrams as a guide ❧

For projects that do not use a core, refer to steps from 19 onwards.
For projects that do not use wool batting, create from roving.

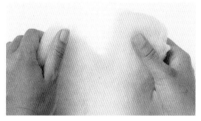

7 Create body. Tease out wool batting, following the direction of the fibers.

8 Tease out even finer, taking a small piece between thumb and forefinger and winding around memory wire for the front leg section, starting at the center.

9 The completed leg will look like this. Repeat for the other leg, again starting from the center and working towards the end.

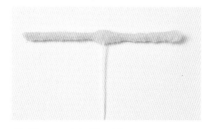

10 The completed front legs.

11 Wrap batting around body section, starting from where it joins to the front legs.

12 The completed core.

13 Add batting to places that look too thin to flesh them out and create shape.

14 Punch randomly all over with the needle to roughly felt in place.

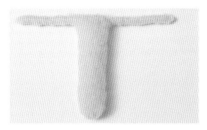

15 The fleshed out core.

16 Bend front legs.

17 Keep adding batting to flesh out places like the chest that may not be full enough.

18 The completed base for the body and front legs.

19 Create face. Tease out batting, then needle in and out to create a ball shape.

20 Roll between the palms of your hands to create a ball about 2 in (5cm) diameter.

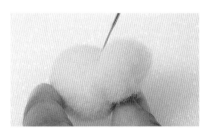

21 Create nose. Take a small amount of batting and punch with needle to attach to head.

22 Smoothing with your fingertips as you go, punch with needle to create shape.

23 The completed nose.

24 In the same way, create base for tail and hind legs from batting.

C Create facial expression 🐾

25 Use needle to create eye holes. Apply adhesive to solid eyes and insert into holes.

26 The completed eyes.

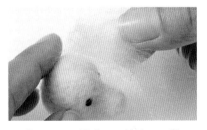

27 Tease out a thin layer of beige and layer around eyes.

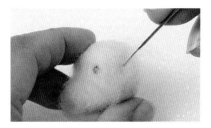

28 Punch through the beige layer to make the shape firm.

29 Create a ball from black roving and punch with needle to tip of nose.

30 Thin out a piece of black roving between your fingers.

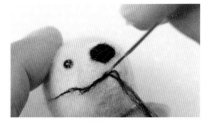

31 Punch mouth into place.

32 When corners of mouth are felted in place, trim off loose ends. Work in the section under the nose in a vertical line.

33 The completed muzzle.

34 Place beige roving over eyes and needle in for eyebrows.

35 Punch to build up areas at outer edges of eyes.

36 Use a small amount of white roving around edges of eyes to create whites of eyes.

D Implant roving on ears and tail 🐾

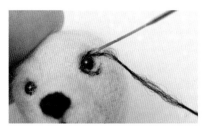

37 Add a fine line of black around the whites of the eyes to create an outline.

38 The finished face.

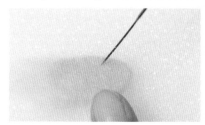

39 Create base of ears from beige roving.

40 Implant roving. Lightly tease out a piece of beige roughly 1⅝ in (4cm) long.

41 Fold in half.

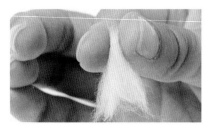

42 Rub the folded section together between two fingers.

43 Spread out the lower part.

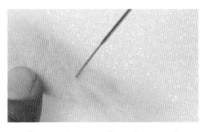

44 Place on lower section of ears and implant by punching in folded section.

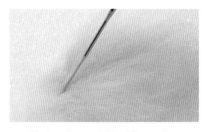

45 Work up the ear bit by bit, creating about four rows.

46 Once four rows are in place, turn ear over and trim off roving that extends outside the base.

47 Trim surface to ¹⁄₁₆ in (2mm) thick.

48 The completed ears. Implant roving into the tail in the same way.

E Attach head to body ❀ *Projects that don't use wool batting use roving instead.*

49 Lightly wrap batting around neck and place head on top.

50 Punch to join head firmly into place, adding layers of batting and working needle in and out firmly as you go.

51 The completed body and head.

F Create claws and paw pads, attach hind legs ❀

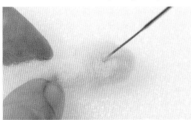

52 Add a layer of beige roving to hind legs to flesh out.

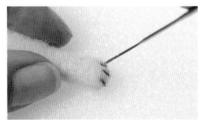

53 Draw out a fine thread of black roving and work in claws.

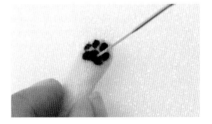

54 Use black roving to create paw pads on undersides of hind feet. Create claws and paw pads in the same way for front feet.

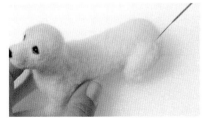

55 Layer batting over body to create haunches.

56 Attach hind legs, felting loosely at joints.

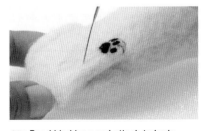

57 Bend hind legs and attach to body.

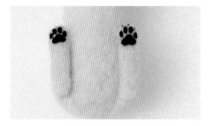

58 The attached hind legs.

59 Side view.

60 Spread out base of tail and attach to body.

61 The tail punched to the body.

H Attach ears 🐾

62 Keeping the overall balance in mind, attach ears to head.

I Implant roving over entire body 🐾

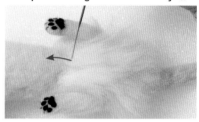

63 Implant roving, starting from the underside of the body near the base of the tail and working upwards. Cut white roving into lengths of about 1⅝ in (4cm), fold in half and needle in at fold.

64 Trim as you implant, neatening roving and making sure the stomach doesn't rise off the ground from too much implanting.

65 Implant beige vertically a little at a time around white on bottom and working up haunches. Trim as you go.

66 The implanting completed on the underside of the body from chest downwards.

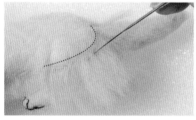

67 Working from the lower back down the sides, implant roving in a fan shape, trimming as you go.

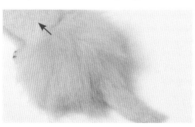

68 The implanting completed from the lower back to the waist. Keep implanting from the back towards the neck.

69 Implant roving from the lower chest working up the neck.

70 Keeping the overall balance in mind, add roving or trim where necessary.

71 Add roving to base of ears and other areas where there are fine joins.

72 The completed figure.

How to create the needle felted animals in this book

Now you're ready to start making cute pets.
The weight, given in grams and ounces, is the approximate amount of wool felt needed.
Lengths are given in inches and metrics. Please note that metric weights
and measurements are more precise.
The size and firmness of the finished project depends on the amount
of punching, so allow more wool felt than you may need.
The order of steps involved may differ from project to project,
but for a general idea refer to the step-by-step instructions on pages 28–32.
For the base, some projects use batting while others use roving. Handle roving that's
used as a base in the same way you'd handle batting.
The basic steps for making the cat figures in this book are the same.
Please refer to pages 54–55 for instructions.

❧ The Japanese Shiba

PAGE 4 **HEIGHT:** 3⅛ in (8cm)

❧ MATERIALS

Roving
  natural blend: light brown 0.07 oz (2g)
  solid: small amounts of white, black
Wool batting—0.21 oz (6g)
Solid eyes ⅛ in (3mm) x 2

1 Create base for each part, referring to full-size
   parts diagrams as a guide

2 Create face and attach ears

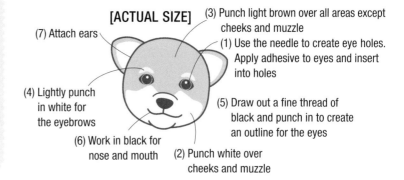

[ACTUAL SIZE]

(7) Attach ears

(3) Punch light brown over all areas except cheeks and muzzle

(1) Use the needle to create eye holes. Apply adhesive to eyes and insert into holes

(4) Lightly punch in white for the eyebrows

(5) Draw out a fine thread of black and punch in to create an outline for the eyes

(6) Work in black for nose and mouth

(2) Punch white over cheeks and muzzle

3 Attach the head on a slight angle to the body

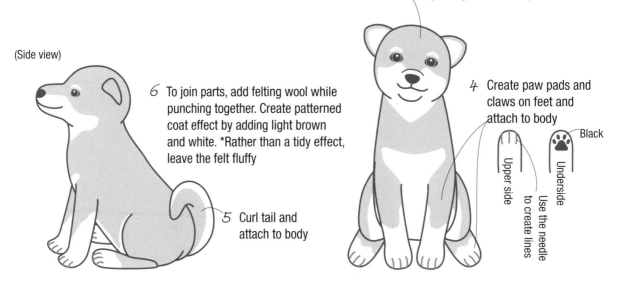

(Side view)

6 To join parts, add felting wool while punching together. Create patterned coat effect by adding light brown and white. *Rather than a tidy effect, leave the felt fluffy

4 Create paw pads and claws on feet and attach to body

Black

Upper side

Underside

Use the needle to create lines

5 Curl tail and attach to body

FULL-SIZE PARTS

Create base from wool batting unless otherwise specified

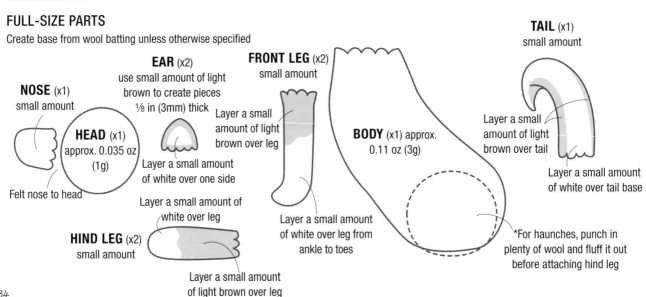

NOSE (x1)
small amount

Felt nose to head

HEAD (x1)
approx. 0.035 oz (1g)

EAR (x2)
use small amount of light brown to create pieces ⅛ in (3mm) thick

Layer a small amount of light brown over leg

Layer a small amount of white over one side

FRONT LEG (x2)
small amount

BODY (x1) approx. 0.11 oz (3g)

TAIL (x1)
small amount

Layer a small amount of light brown over tail

Layer a small amount of white over tail base

Layer a small amount of white over leg

HIND LEG (x2)
small amount

Layer a small amount of light brown over leg

Layer a small amount of white over leg from ankle to toes

*For haunches, punch in plenty of wool and fluff it out before attaching hind leg

♣ The Hokkaido Dog

PAGE 5   **HEIGHT:** 3½ in (9cm)

♣ MATERIALS

Roving
   solid: white 0.14 oz (4g); small amounts of black
   natural blend: small amounts of light brown
Wool batting—0.28 oz (8g)
Solid eyes ⅛ in (3mm) x 2
Florist wire—7½ in (19cm)

1 Using florist wire to form the core, create base for body and front legs as per the Golden Retriever pup on p28, referring to the full-size parts diagram as a guide
   *Use 3⅛ in (8cm) of florist wire for the body and 4⅜ in (11cm) for the front legs

2 Create base for each part, referring to full-size parts diagrams as a guide

3 Create face and attach ears

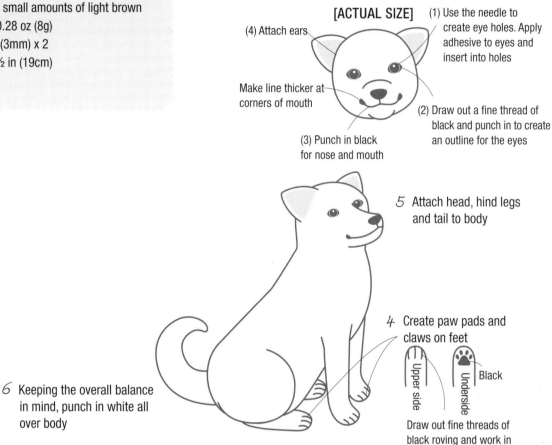

[ACTUAL SIZE]

(4) Attach ears

(1) Use the needle to create eye holes. Apply adhesive to eyes and insert into holes

Make line thicker at corners of mouth

(2) Draw out a fine thread of black and punch in to create an outline for the eyes

(3) Punch in black for nose and mouth

5 Attach head, hind legs and tail to body

4 Create paw pads and claws on feet

Upper side

Underside

Black

Draw out fine threads of black roving and work in

6 Keeping the overall balance in mind, punch in white all over body

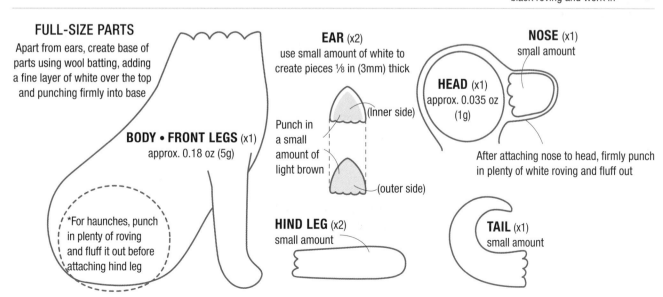

FULL-SIZE PARTS

Apart from ears, create base of parts using wool batting, adding a fine layer of white over the top and punching firmly into base

BODY • FRONT LEGS (x1)
approx. 0.18 oz (5g)

*For haunches, punch in plenty of roving and fluff it out before attaching hind leg

EAR (x2)
use small amount of white to create pieces ⅛ in (3mm) thick

(Inner side)

Punch in a small amount of light brown

(outer side)

NOSE (x1)
small amount

HEAD (x1)
approx. 0.035 oz (1g)

After attaching nose to head, firmly punch in plenty of white roving and fluff out

HIND LEG (x2)
small amount

TAIL (x1)
small amount

♣ Miniature Dachshund

PAGE 6 **LENGTH:** 6¼ in (16cm)

♣ MATERIALS

Roving
  solid: black 0.25 oz (7g); small amount of white
  natural blend: small amount of light brown
Wool batting—0.25 oz (7g)
Solid eyes ⅛ in (3mm) x 2
Florist wire—3½ in (9cm)

1 Referring to the full-size parts diagram, use florist wire to form the base and create front legs. Attach legs to body

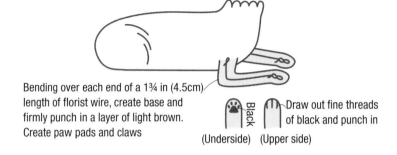

Bending over each end of a 1¾ in (4.5cm) length of florist wire, create base and firmly punch in a layer of light brown. Create paw pads and claws

(Underside)   (Upper side)

Black   Draw out fine threads of black and punch in

2 Create base for each part, referring to full-size parts diagram as a guide

3 Create face. Once roving has been added to the ears, attach them to the head

[ACTUAL SIZE]

(3) Punch in black for all areas of the face, except for cheeks and muzzle

(4) Punch in light brown for eyebrows

(2) Punch in light brown for muzzle

(1) Use the needle to create eye holes. Apply adhesive to eyes and insert into holes

(5) Punch in white under eyes to create the appearance of raised eyes

(6) Punch in black for nose and mouth

(7) Punch black into ear base, referring to the dotted lines and numbers in the diagram as a guide for positioning and order of work. Trim short with scissors, neaten to give the look of naturally flowing hair, and attach to head

③ ② ①

(Underside)

Implant white and light brown roving, working from the belly and base of tail towards the head and keeping in mind the natural direction that hair grows. Work black in for the back. Check the overall effect as you work, trimming where necessary. Repeat until the entire body has been covered

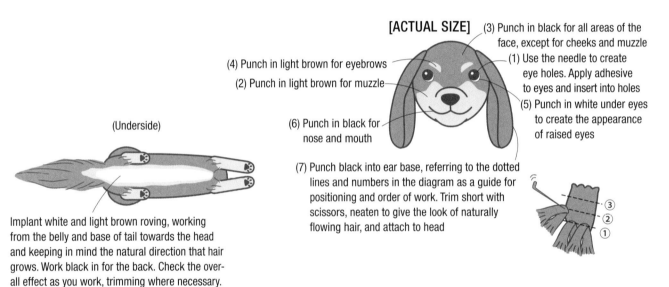

7 Add wool batting as you work when joining parts. Implant hair over entire body

6 Implant black roving on tail and attach to body

4 Attach head to body on an angle to give the effect of looking up

Implant light brown roving on chest to create markings

5 Create paw pads and claws on hind feet and attach legs to body

FULL-SIZE PARTS

Use wool batting to create base for all parts except ears

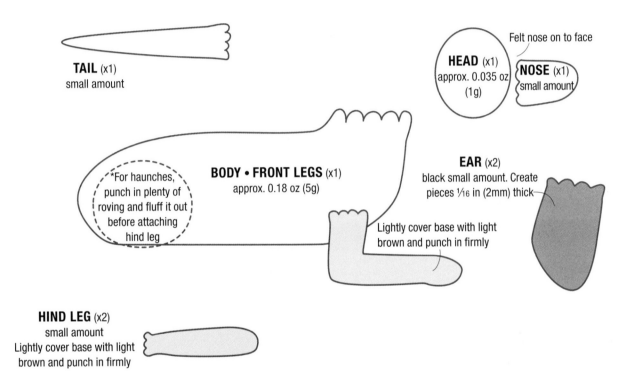

TAIL (x1)
small amount

Felt nose on to face

HEAD (x1)
approx. 0.035 oz
(1g)

NOSE (x1)
small amount

BODY • FRONT LEGS (x1)
approx. 0.18 oz (5g)

*For haunches, punch in plenty of roving and fluff it out before attaching hind leg

Lightly cover base with light brown and punch in firmly

EAR (x2)
black small amount. Create pieces ¹⁄₁₆ in (2mm) thick

HIND LEG (x2)
small amount
Lightly cover base with light brown and punch in firmly

❧ The Chihuahua

PAGE 6 HEIGHT: 4 in (10cm)

❧ MATERIALS

Roving
  solid: black 0.18 oz (5g); small amounts
  each of white, beige , salmon pink
  mix: small amount of khaki
Wool batting—0.28 oz (8g)
Glass eyes ⅛ in (4mm) x 2
Florist wire—7¼ in (18.5cm)

1 Using florist wire to form the core, create base for body and front legs as per the Golden Retriever pup on p28 referring to the full-size parts diagram as a guide.

   *Use 3 in (7.5cm) of florist wire for the body and 4⅜ in (11cm) for the front legs

2 Create base for each part, referring to full-size parts diagrams as a guide

3 Create face and attach ears

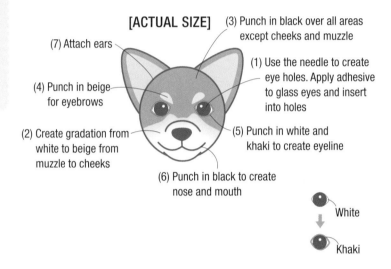

[ACTUAL SIZE]

(7) Attach ears

(3) Punch in black over all areas except cheeks and muzzle

(4) Punch in beige for eyebrows

(1) Use the needle to create eye holes. Apply adhesive to glass eyes and insert into holes

(2) Create gradation from white to beige from muzzle to cheeks

(5) Punch in white and khaki to create eyeline

(6) Punch in black to create nose and mouth

White
Khaki

Implant roving, working from the lower part of the belly and keeping in mind the natural direction that hair grows. Work white in for the lower part of the belly and inner haunches, using black for the rest of the body. Check the overall effect as you work, trimming where necessary. Repeat until the entire body has been covered

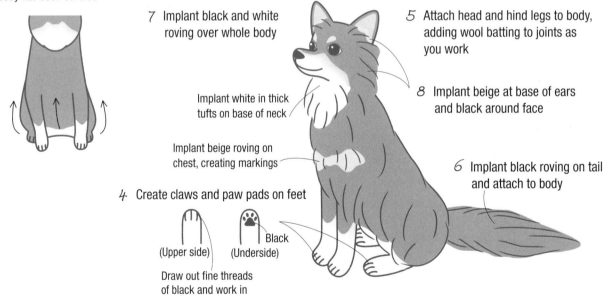

7 Implant black and white roving over whole body

Implant white in thick tufts on base of neck

Implant beige roving on chest, creating markings

4 Create claws and paw pads on feet

(Upper side) (Underside) Black

Draw out fine threads of black and work in

5 Attach head and hind legs to body, adding wool batting to joints as you work

8 Implant beige at base of ears and black around face

6 Implant black roving on tail and attach to body

FULL-SIZE PARTS

Use wool batting to create base for all parts except ears

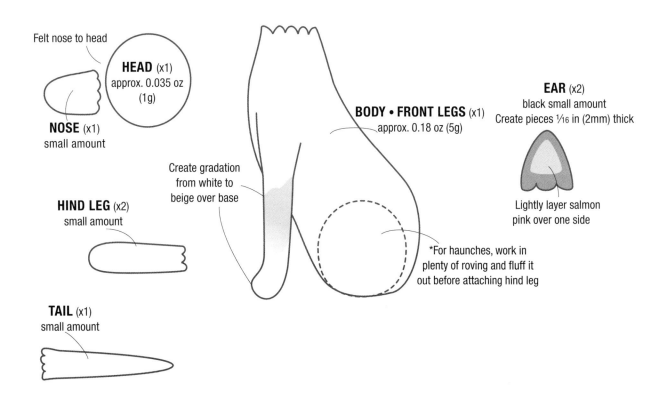

Felt nose to head

HEAD (x1)
approx. 0.035 oz
(1g)

NOSE (x1)
small amount

EAR (x2)
black small amount
Create pieces ¹⁄₁₆ in (2mm) thick

BODY • FRONT LEGS (x1)
approx. 0.18 oz (5g)

Lightly layer salmon
pink over one side

Create gradation
from white to
beige over base

HIND LEG (x2)
small amount

*For haunches, work in
plenty of roving and fluff it
out before attaching hind leg

TAIL (x1)
small amount

♣ Rabbits

PAGE 7 **STANDING FIGURE: HEIGHT:** 4⅜ in (11cm);
PRONE FIGURE: LENGTH: 2¾ in (7cm)

♣ MATERIALS

(FOR STANDING FIGURE)
Roving
  mix: khaki 0.7 oz (20g)
  natural blend: pink 0.007 oz (0.2g)
  solid: small amounts each of black, beige,
  dark brown
Semi-spherical button with shank ¼ in (6mm) x 2

(FOR PRONE FIGURE)
Roving
  colored wool: blue-faced Leicester 0.39 oz (11g)
  solid: 0.0035 oz (0.1g) each of beige and dark brown;
  small amount of black
Solid eyes ¼ in (5mm) x 2

1 Create parts, referring to full-size parts diagram as a reference

2 Create face

<STANDING FIGURE: ACTUAL SIZE>

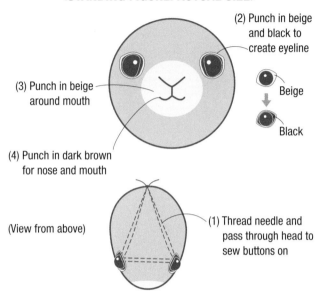

(2) Punch in beige
and black to
create eyeline

(3) Punch in beige
around mouth

Beige

Black

(4) Punch in dark brown
for nose and mouth

(View from above)

(1) Thread needle and
pass through head to
sew buttons on

<PRONE FIGURE: ACTUAL SIZE>

(1) Use awl to create eye
holes. Apply adhesive
to solid eyes and
insert into holes

(2) Punch in beige and
black to create eyeline

Beige

Black

(3) Punch in dark brown
to separate puffed-up
area around mouth
into two

(4) Punch in black in line
with puffed-up area
around mouth to create
nose and mouth

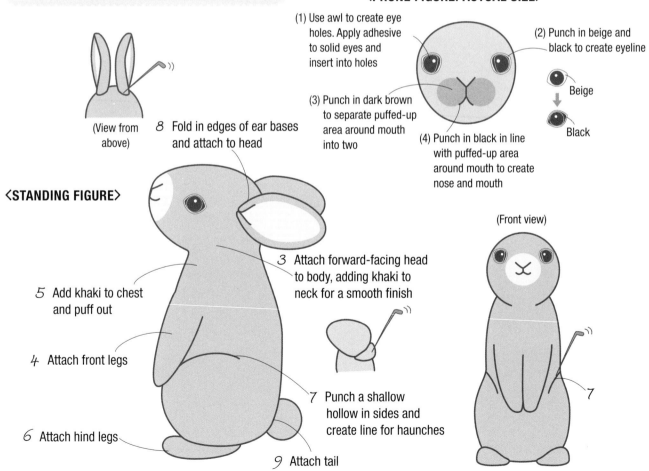

(View from
above)

8 Fold in edges of ear bases
and attach to head

<STANDING FIGURE>

5 Add khaki to chest
and puff out

4 Attach front legs

6 Attach hind legs

3 Attach forward-facing head
to body, adding khaki to
neck for a smooth finish

7 Punch a shallow
hollow in sides and
create line for haunches

9 Attach tail

(Front view)

7

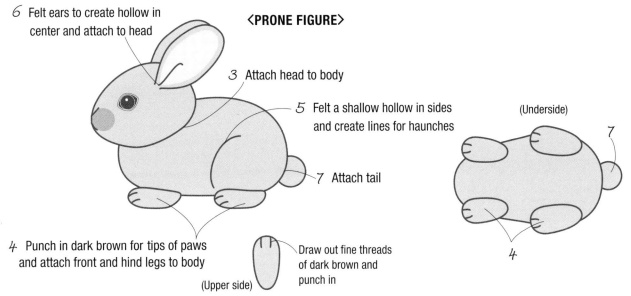

6 Felt ears to create hollow in center and attach to head

⟨PRONE FIGURE⟩

3 Attach head to body

5 Felt a shallow hollow in sides and create lines for haunches

(Underside)

7

7 Attach tail

4 Punch in dark brown for tips of paws and attach front and hind legs to body

Draw out fine threads of dark brown and punch in

(Upper side)

4

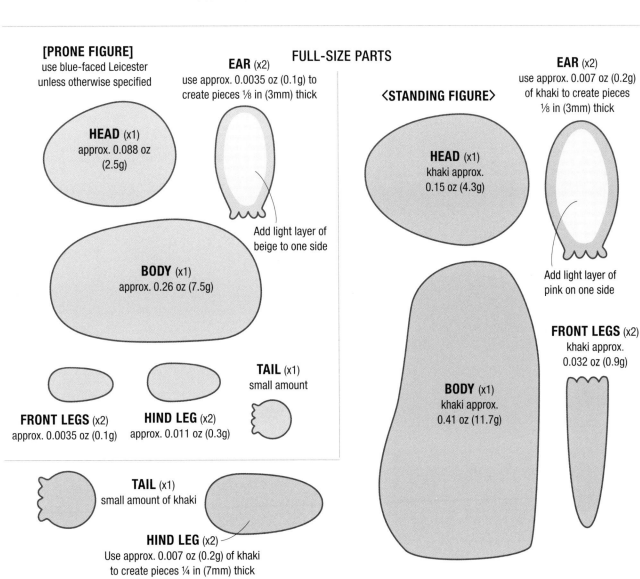

[PRONE FIGURE]
use blue-faced Leicester unless otherwise specified

FULL-SIZE PARTS

EAR (x2)
use approx. 0.0035 oz (0.1g) to create pieces ⅛ in (3mm) thick

HEAD (x1)
approx. 0.088 oz (2.5g)

Add light layer of beige to one side

BODY (x1)
approx. 0.26 oz (7.5g)

TAIL (x1)
small amount

FRONT LEGS (x2)
approx. 0.0035 oz (0.1g)

HIND LEG (x2)
approx. 0.011 oz (0.3g)

TAIL (x1)
small amount of khaki

HIND LEG (x2)
Use approx. 0.007 oz (0.2g) of khaki to create pieces ¼ in (7mm) thick

⟨STANDING FIGURE⟩

HEAD (x1)
khaki approx. 0.15 oz (4.3g)

EAR (x2)
use approx. 0.007 oz (0.2g) of khaki to create pieces ⅛ in (3mm) thick

Add light layer of pink on one side

FRONT LEGS (x2)
khaki approx. 0.032 oz (0.9g)

BODY (x1)
khaki approx. 0.41 oz (11.7g)

❧ Golden Retriever

PAGE 8   **PUPPY LENGTH:** 6¼ in (16cm)
PARENT HEIGHT: 4½ in (11.5cm)

❧ MATERIALS

(PUPPY)
Roving
   solid: beige 0.21 oz (6g); small amounts each
   of white, black
Wool batting—0.25 oz (7g)
Solid eyes ⅛ in (3mm) x 2
Florist wire—9⅝ in (24.5cm)

(PARENT DOG)
Roving
   solid: beige 0.35 oz (10g); small amounts each
   of white, black
Wool batting—0.28 oz (8g)
Solid eyes ⅛ in (3mm) x 2
Florist wire—8¼ in (21cm)

※ Please refer to the process lesson on p28–32
for detailed instructions on making the puppy.
The parent dog is made in the same way.

1 Create base for body and front legs from florist wire

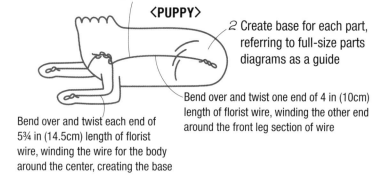

〈PUPPY〉

2 Create base for each part, referring to full-size parts diagrams as a guide

Bend over and twist one end of 4 in (10cm) length of florist wire, winding the other end around the front leg section of wire

Bend over and twist each end of 5¾ in (14.5cm) length of florist wire, winding the wire for the body around the center, creating the base

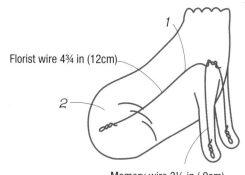

〈PARENT DOG〉

Florist wire 4¾ in (12cm)

Memory wire 3½ in (9cm)

3 Create expression on face

〈PUPPY: ACTUAL SIZE〉

(3) Layer beige over eyes and punch in to create eyebrows. Use a small amount of white to create whites of eyes

(4) Draw out a fine thread of black and punch in to create an outline for the eyes and give the appearance of looking up

(1) Use the needle to create eye holes. Apply adhesive to solid eyes and insert into holes. Layer beige around eyes and punch in

(2) Punch in black to create nose and mouth

Make mouth thicker at corners

〈PARENT DOG—ACTUAL SIZE〉
Create facial expression in the same way as for puppy

Layer beige over eyes and punch in

Draw out a fine thread of black and punch in to create an outline for the eyes

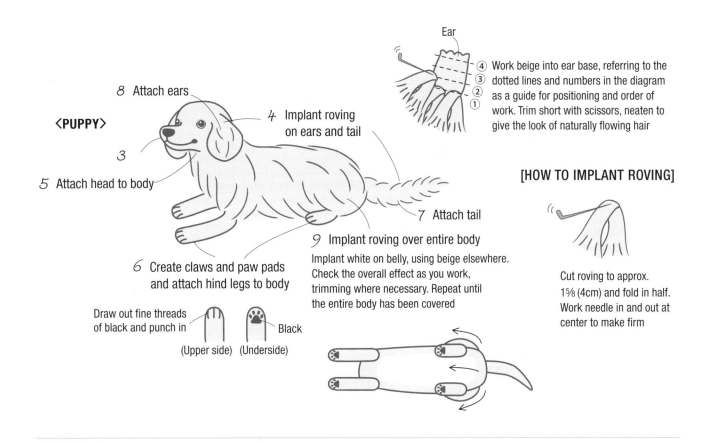

Ear

④ Work beige into ear base, referring to the
③ dotted lines and numbers in the diagram
② as a guide for positioning and order of
① work. Trim short with scissors, neaten to
give the look of naturally flowing hair

<PUPPY>

8 Attach ears

4 Implant roving
on ears and tail

3

5 Attach head to body

7 Attach tail

9 Implant roving over entire body

Implant white on belly, using beige elsewhere.
Check the overall effect as you work,
trimming where necessary. Repeat until
the entire body has been covered

6 Create claws and paw pads
and attach hind legs to body

Draw out fine threads
of black and punch in

Black

(Upper side) (Underside)

[HOW TO IMPLANT ROVING]

Cut roving to approx.
1⅝ (4cm) and fold in half.
Work needle in and out at
center to make firm

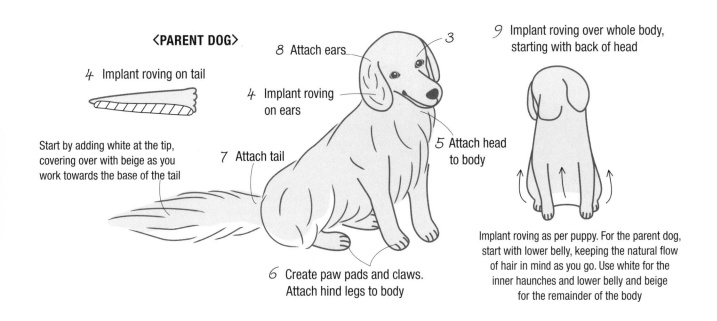

<PARENT DOG>

4 Implant roving on tail

8 Attach ears

3

9 Implant roving over whole body,
starting with back of head

4 Implant roving
on ears

5 Attach head
to body

Start by adding white at the tip,
covering over with beige as you
work towards the base of the tail

7 Attach tail

6 Create paw pads and claws.
Attach hind legs to body

Implant roving as per puppy. For the parent dog,
start with lower belly, keeping the natural flow
of hair in mind as you go. Use white for the
inner haunches and lower belly and beige
for the remainder of the body

43

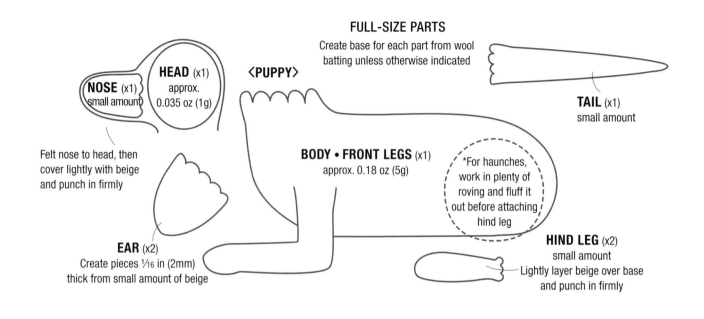

FULL-SIZE PARTS

Create base for each part from wool batting unless otherwise indicated

NOSE (x1)
small amount

HEAD (x1)
approx.
0.035 oz (1g)

<PUPPY>

TAIL (x1)
small amount

Felt nose to head, then cover lightly with beige and punch in firmly

BODY • FRONT LEGS (x1)
approx. 0.18 oz (5g)

*For haunches, work in plenty of roving and fluff it out before attaching hind leg

EAR (x2)
Create pieces 1/16 in (2mm) thick from small amount of beige

HIND LEG (x2)
small amount
Lightly layer beige over base and punch in firmly

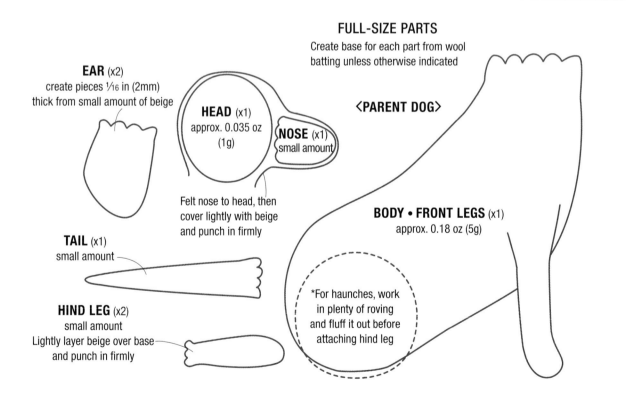

FULL-SIZE PARTS

Create base for each part from wool batting unless otherwise indicated

EAR (x2)
create pieces 1/16 in (2mm) thick from small amount of beige

HEAD (x1)
approx. 0.035 oz (1g)

NOSE (x1)
small amount

<PARENT DOG>

Felt nose to head, then cover lightly with beige and punch in firmly

BODY • FRONT LEGS (x1)
approx. 0.18 oz (5g)

TAIL (x1)
small amount

HIND LEG (x2)
small amount
Lightly layer beige over base and punch in firmly

*For haunches, work in plenty of roving and fluff it out before attaching hind leg

♣ Labrador Retriever

PAGE 9 **HEIGHT:** 4⅜ in (11cm)

♣ MATERIALS
Roving
  solid: beige 0.11 oz (3g); small amount of black
Wool batting—0.28 oz (8g)
Solid eyes ⅛ in (3mm) x 2
Florist wire—8¼ in (21cm)

1 Use florist wire to create body and front legs base as per Golden
Retriever puppy on p28, referring to full-size parts diagram as a guide.
*Use 3½ in (9cm) of memory wire for body and 4¾ in (12cm) for front legs

2 Create base for each part, referring to full-size parts diagrams as a guide

3 Create head

[ACTUAL SIZE]

(1) Use the needle to create eye holes.
Apply adhesive to solid eyes
and insert into holes. Layer
beige around eyes and
punch in

Make mouth thicker at corners

(3) Punch in black for
nose and mouth

(2) Draw out a fine
thread of black and
punch in to create
an outline for the eyes

5 Attach head, hind legs and
tail to body. Attach ears to
head. For joints, work in
wool batting as you go

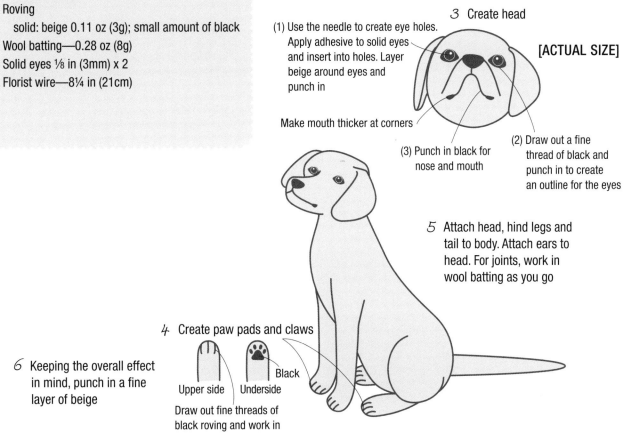

4 Create paw pads and claws

Black

Upper side   Underside

Draw out fine threads of
black roving and work in

6 Keeping the overall effect
in mind, punch in a fine
layer of beige

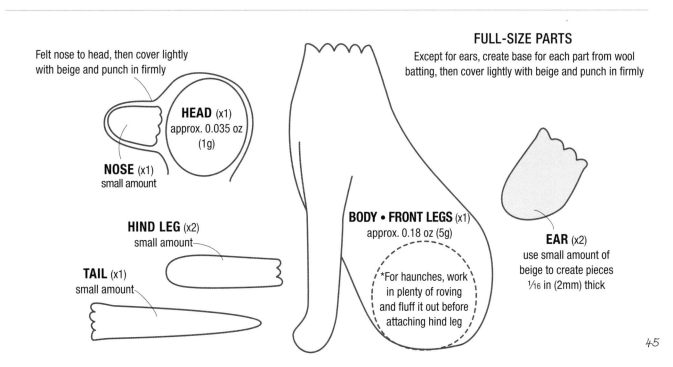

Felt nose to head, then cover lightly
with beige and punch in firmly

HEAD (x1)
approx. 0.035 oz
(1g)

NOSE (x1)
small amount

FULL-SIZE PARTS
Except for ears, create base for each part from wool
batting, then cover lightly with beige and punch in firmly

HIND LEG (x2)
small amount

TAIL (x1)
small amount

BODY • FRONT LEGS (x1)
approx. 0.18 oz (5g)

*For haunches, work
in plenty of roving
and fluff it out before
attaching hind leg

EAR (x2)
use small amount of
beige to create pieces
1/16 in (2mm) thick

🐾 Toy Poodle

PAGE 10 **HEIGHT:** 2⅛ in (5.5cm)

🐾 MATERIALS

Roving
   mix: beige 0.13 oz (3.8g)
   natural blend: small amounts each of dark
   brown, pink
Solid eyes ⅛ in (3mm) x 3

1 Create each part, referring to full-size parts diagram as a guide

2 Create face. Attach ears and decorations

(1) Use the needle to create eye holes.
    Apply adhesive to solid eyes and
    insert into holes

[ACTUAL SIZE]

(3) Add beige to fill
out forehead

(2) Punch in dark brown for mouth

(Side view)

(4) Felt ears to sides of head

(5) Make pink balls and punch in

3 Attach head to body, attach front legs

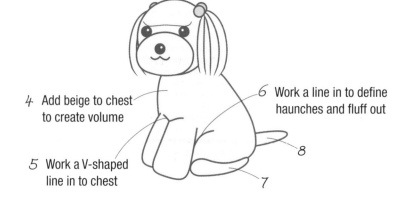

4 Add beige to chest
to create volume

5 Work a V-shaped
line in to chest

6 Work a line in to define
haunches and fluff out

8

7

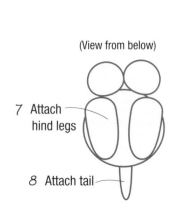

(View from below)

7 Attach
hind legs

8 Attach tail

FULL-SIZE PARTS

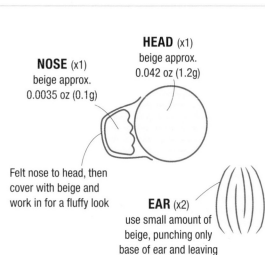

NOSE (x1)
beige approx.
0.0035 oz (0.1g)

HEAD (x1)
beige approx.
0.042 oz (1.2g)

Felt nose to head, then
cover with beige and
work in for a fluffy look

EAR (x2)
use small amount of
beige, punching only
base of ear and leaving
the rest as loose wool

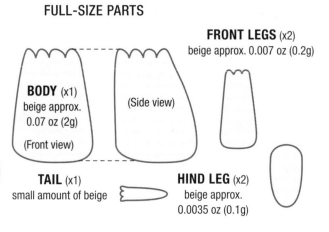

BODY (x1)
beige approx.
0.07 oz (2g)

(Front view)

(Side view)

FRONT LEGS (x2)
beige approx. 0.007 oz (0.2g)

TAIL (x1)
small amount of beige

HIND LEG (x2)
beige approx.
0.0035 oz (0.1g)

❧ The Pomeranian

PAGE 10 **HEIGHT:** 2 in (5cm)

❧ MATERIALS

Roving

    natural blend: light brown 0.13 oz (3.6g);

    small amount of pink

    mix: beige 0.014 oz (0.4g)

    solid: small amount of black

Solid eyes ⅛ in (3mm) x 3

FULL-SIZE PARTS

EAR (x2)
use small amount of light brown
to create pieces ⅛ in (3mm) thick

Add a light
layer of pink

HEAD (x1)
light brown approx.
0.028 oz (0.8g)

NOSE (x1)
small amount of
light brown

Felt nose to head

TONGUE (x1)
use small amount of pink to
create piece 1/16 in (2mm) thick

BODY (x1)
light brown approx.
0.07 oz (2g)

LEG (x4)
light brown approx.
0.0035 oz (0.1g)

TAIL (x1)
beige approx. 0.011 oz (0.3g)

---

1 Create each part, referring to full-size parts diagram as a guide

2 Create face

[ACTUAL SIZE]

(1) Use the needle to create
eye holes. Apply adhesive
to solid eyes and insert
into holes

(3) Attach tongue

(2) Draw out a fine thread
of black and punch in
for mouth

3 Attach head and legs to body

Attach head on
a slight angle

Attach legs

4 Add to body
and fluff out

Add light brown from behind
head over body, working through
to create a full, fluffy coat

6 Add light brown to cheeks, punching
to create a full, fluffy effect

7 Attach ears

Add light brown over beige
on chest and punch in for
a fluffy effect

5 Add beige to chest, punching
in to create a full, fluffy effect

8 Curl tail and felt firmly to
body, at the same time
creating a fluffy effect

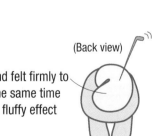

(Back view)

♣ The Pug

PAGE 10   **HEIGHT:** 1¼ in (3cm)

♣ MATERIALS
Roving
   natural blend: beige 0.11 oz (3.2g), small
   amounts each of light brown, dark grey
   mix: black 0.0035 oz (0.1g)
   solid: small amount of black
Solid eyes ⅛ in (4mm) x 2

FULL-SIZE PARTS

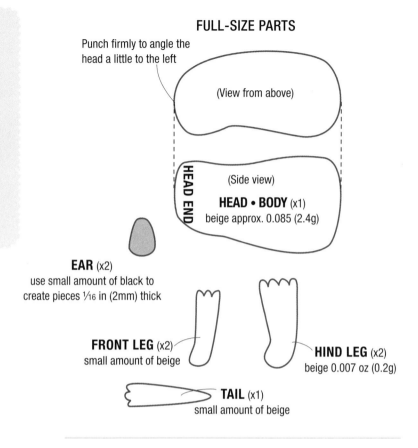

Punch firmly to angle the head a little to the left

(View from above)

HEAD END

(Side view)
HEAD • BODY (x1)
beige approx. 0.085 (2.4g)

EAR (x2)
use small amount of black to
create pieces ¹⁄₁₆ in (2mm) thick

FRONT LEG (x2)
small amount of beige

HIND LEG (x2)
beige 0.007 oz (0.2g)

TAIL (x1)
small amount of beige

1 Create each part, referring to full-size parts diagram as a guide

2 Create face

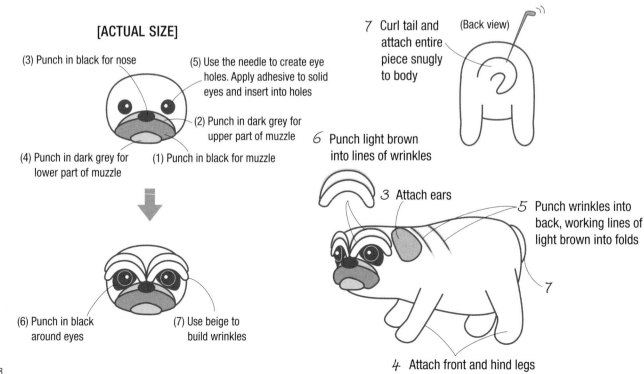

[ACTUAL SIZE]

(3) Punch in black for nose

(5) Use the needle to create eye holes. Apply adhesive to solid eyes and insert into holes

(2) Punch in dark grey for upper part of muzzle

(4) Punch in dark grey for lower part of muzzle

(1) Punch in black for muzzle

(6) Punch in black around eyes

(7) Use beige to build wrinkles

7 Curl tail and attach entire piece snugly to body

(Back view)

6 Punch light brown into lines of wrinkles

3 Attach ears

5 Punch wrinkles into back, working lines of light brown into folds

7

4 Attach front and hind legs

48

🐾 The Dachshund

PAGE 10   **HEIGHT:** 2⅛ in (5.5cm)

🐾 MATERIALS

Roving

   solid: black 0.095 oz (2.7g), pale blue
0.007 oz (0.2g)

   mix: red brown 0.021 oz (0.6g)

Solid eyes ⅛ in (4mm) x 2

1 Create each part, referring to full-size parts diagram as a guide

2 Create face, attach ears

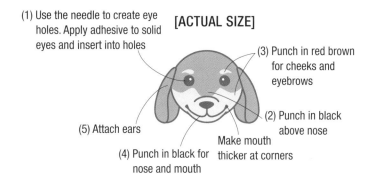

(1) Use the needle to create eye holes. Apply adhesive to solid eyes and insert into holes

[ACTUAL SIZE]

(3) Punch in red brown for cheeks and eyebrows

(2) Punch in black above nose

(5) Attach ears

Make mouth thicker at corners

(4) Punch in black for nose and mouth

3 Attach head, front legs and hind legs to body

[HOW TO ATTACH TIE AND KNOT DETAIL]

With the bandanna positioned at the front, attach the tie from the side in line with the neck

(Back view)

Punch through knot at center to attach

(Front view)

6 Attach bandanna, tie and knot

5 Attach tail

[ACTUAL SIZE]

4 Create markings on chest using red brown

Create markings using red brown

Attach legs, working through black at joining sections

FULL-SIZE PARTS

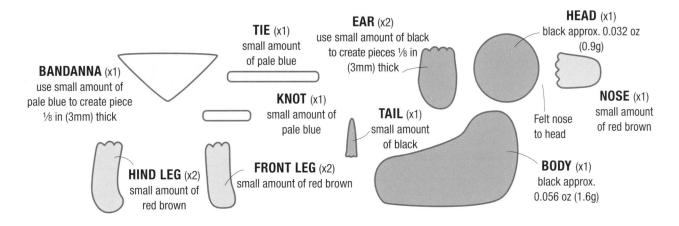

BANDANNA (x1)
use small amount of pale blue to create piece ⅛ in (3mm) thick

TIE (x1)
small amount of pale blue

KNOT (x1)
small amount of pale blue

EAR (x2)
use small amount of black to create pieces ⅛ in (3mm) thick

TAIL (x1)
small amount of black

HEAD (x1)
black approx. 0.032 oz (0.9g)

Felt nose to head

NOSE (x1)
small amount of red brown

BODY (x1)
black approx. 0.056 oz (1.6g)

HIND LEG (x2)
small amount of red brown

FRONT LEG (x2)
small amount of red brown

♣ Shih Tzu

PAGE 11   **HEIGHT:** 3⅛ in (8cm)

♣ MATERIALS

Roving
  natural blend: white 0.42 oz (12g)
  mix: khaki 0.025 oz (0.7g)
  solid: small amount of black
Solid eyes ¼ in (5mm) x 2

1 Create each part, referring to full-size parts diagram as a guide

2 Create face

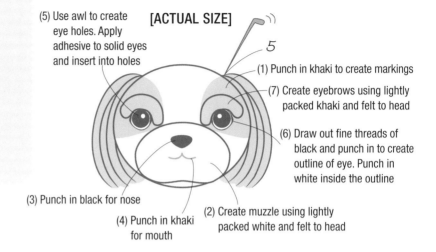

(5) Use awl to create eye holes. Apply adhesive to solid eyes and insert into holes

[ACTUAL SIZE]

5

(1) Punch in khaki to create markings

(7) Create eyebrows using lightly packed khaki and felt to head

(6) Draw out fine threads of black and punch in to create outline of eye. Punch in white inside the outline

(3) Punch in black for nose

(4) Punch in khaki for mouth

(2) Create muzzle using lightly packed white and felt to head

3 Attach head, front legs and hind legs to body

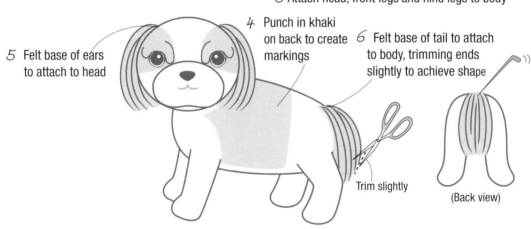

5 Felt base of ears to attach to head

4 Punch in khaki on back to create markings

6 Felt base of tail to attach to body, trimming ends slightly to achieve shape

Trim slightly

(Back view)

FULL-SIZE PARTS

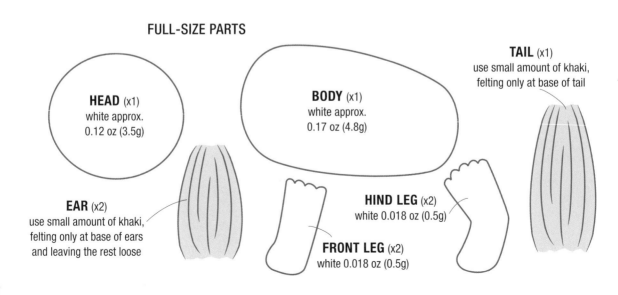

HEAD (x1)
white approx.
0.12 oz (3.5g)

BODY (x1)
white approx.
0.17 oz (4.8g)

TAIL (x1)
use small amount of khaki,
felting only at base of tail

EAR (x2)
use small amount of khaki,
felting only at base of ears
and leaving the rest loose

FRONT LEG (x2)
white 0.018 oz (0.5g)

HIND LEG (x2)
white 0.018 oz (0.5g)

♣ Welsh Terrier (Airedale)

PAGE 12   **HEIGHT:** 4 in (10cm)

♣ MATERIALS

Roving
  natural blend: light brown 0.49 oz (14g)
  mix: black 0.042 oz (1.2g)
  solid: small amount of dark grey
solid eyes ⅛ in (4mm) x 2

1 Create each part, referring to full-size parts diagram as a guide

2 Create face and attach ears

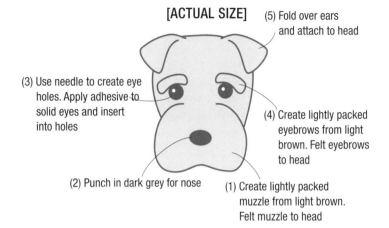

[ACTUAL SIZE]

(5) Fold over ears and attach to head

(3) Use needle to create eye holes. Apply adhesive to solid eyes and insert into holes

(4) Create lightly packed eyebrows from light brown. Felt eyebrows to head

(2) Punch in dark grey for nose

(1) Create lightly packed muzzle from light brown. Felt muzzle to head

3 Attach front legs and high legs to body. Join body and head by felting each part to neck

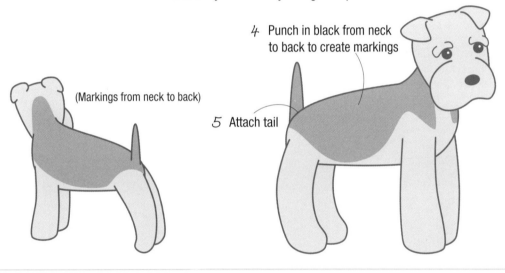

4 Punch in black from neck to back to create markings

(Markings from neck to back)

5 Attach tail

FULL-SIZE PARTS

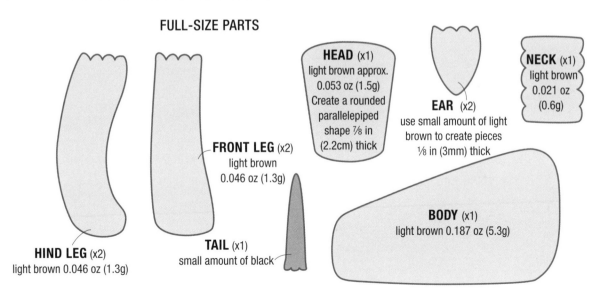

FRONT LEG (x2)
light brown
0.046 oz (1.3g)

HEAD (x1)
light brown approx.
0.053 oz (1.5g)
Create a rounded
parallelepiped
shape ⅞ in
(2.2cm) thick

EAR (x2)
use small amount of light
brown to create pieces
⅛ in (3mm) thick

NECK (x1)
light brown
0.021 oz
(0.6g)

HIND LEG (x2)
light brown 0.046 oz (1.3g)

TAIL (x1)
small amount of black

BODY (x1)
light brown 0.187 oz (5.3g)

🐾 Siamese Cat

PAGE 13 **HEIGHT:** 4 in (10cm)

🐾 MATERIALS
Roving
   natural blend: white 0.35 oz (10g)
   mix: small amount of beige
   solid: small amounts of black and dark brown
Plastic eyes ⅜ in (9mm), blue x 2
Florist wire—7⅞ in (20cm)
Fishing line (size 2)—12⅝ in (32cm)

1 Create each part, referring to full-size parts diagram as a guide

2 Create face and attach ears

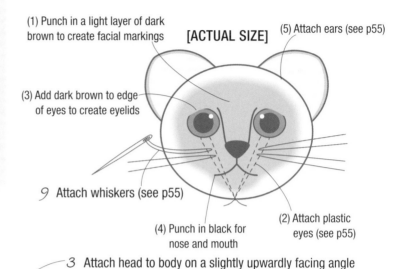

(1) Punch in a light layer of dark brown to create facial markings

[ACTUAL SIZE]

(5) Attach ears (see p55)

(3) Add dark brown to edge of eyes to create eyelids

9 Attach whiskers (see p55)

(4) Punch in black for nose and mouth

(2) Attach plastic eyes (see p55)

3 Attach head to body on a slightly upwardly facing angle

7 Add white to area where front legs join body and blend in to body

Bend up front left paw to create pose

8 Attach tail to body in same way as front legs

5 Add white to haunches and fluff out

6 At points where front legs joins body, use needle to create holes. Bend ends of florist wire, apply adhesive and insert

4 Flatten out underside so cat stays upright without support. Attach hind legs

---

FULL-SIZE PARTS
Use florist wire at core of front legs and tail (see p55)

HEAD (x1)
white approx. 0.11 oz (3g)

*See p54 for how to make head

EAR (x2)
using small amount of beige, create pieces ⅛ in (3mm) thick

(Inner side)

(Outer side)

Lightly layer dark brown over top

TAIL (x1)
small amount of dark brown

HIND LEG (x2)
small amount of dark brown

Florist wire 2⅜ in (6cm)

FRONT LEGS (x2)
small amount of white

Create gradation from dark brown to beige over the top of white

Florist wire 3⅛ in (8cm)

BODY (x1)
white approx. 0.18 oz (5g)

(Side view)
Attach front leg here

First, create a large and a small ball, then wind around with roving to form body (from the front, it will look like a gourd shape)

Attach tail here

52

✤ The American Tabby

PAGE 14 **HEIGHT:** 4¼ in (10.5cm)

✤ MATERIALS

Roving
  natural blend: white 0.35 oz (10g),
  grey 0.11 oz (3g), dark grey 0.07 oz (2g);
  small amounts each of dark brown and pink
Solid: small amount of black
Plastic eyes ⅜ in (9mm) green x 2
Florist wire—7⅞ in (20cm)
Fishing line (size 2)—12⅝ in (32cm)

1 Create each part, referring to full-size parts diagram as a guide

2 Create face and attach ears

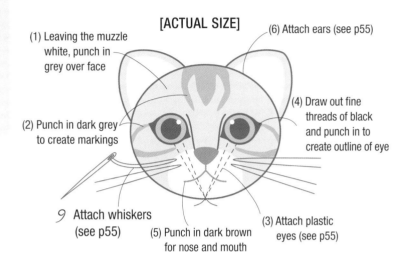

[ACTUAL SIZE]

(1) Leaving the muzzle white, punch in grey over face

(6) Attach ears (see p55)

(2) Punch in dark grey to create markings

(4) Draw out fine threads of black and punch in to create outline of eye

9 Attach whiskers (see p55)

(5) Punch in dark brown for nose and mouth

(3) Attach plastic eyes (see p55)

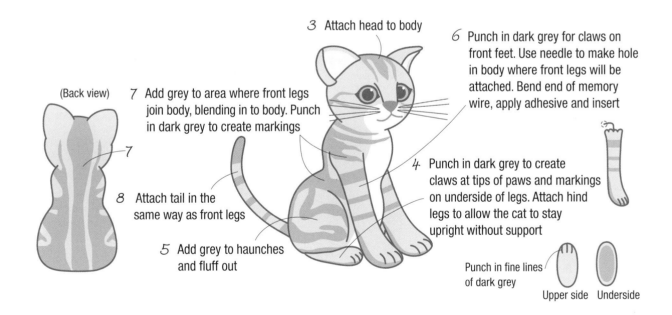

3 Attach head to body

6 Punch in dark grey for claws on front feet. Use needle to make hole in body where front legs will be attached. Bend end of memory wire, apply adhesive and insert

(Back view)

7 Add grey to area where front legs join body, blending in to body. Punch in dark grey to create markings

7

8 Attach tail in the same way as front legs

4 Punch in dark grey to create claws at tips of paws and markings on underside of legs. Attach hind legs to allow the cat to stay upright without support

5 Add grey to haunches and fluff out

Punch in fine lines of dark grey

Upper side   Underside

FULL-SIZE PARTS

Create core for front legs and
tail from florist wire (see p55)

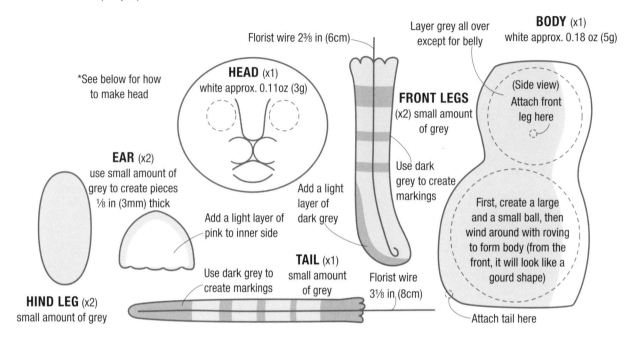

*See below for how
to make head

HEAD (x1)
white approx. 0.11oz (3g)

EAR (x2)
use small amount of
grey to create pieces
⅛ in (3mm) thick

Add a light layer of
pink to inner side

HIND LEG (x2)
small amount of grey

Use dark grey to
create markings

TAIL (x1)
small amount
of grey

Add a light
layer of
dark grey

Florist wire 2⅜ in (6cm)

Layer grey all over
except for belly

FRONT LEGS
(x2) small amount
of grey

Use dark
grey to create
markings

Florist wire
3⅛ in (8cm)

BODY (x1)
white approx. 0.18 oz (5g)

(Side view)
Attach front
leg here

First, create a large
and a small ball, then
wind around with roving
to form body (from the
front, it will look like a
gourd shape)

Attach tail here

Basic steps for creating cats on p52-62

[HOW TO MAKE THE HEAD]

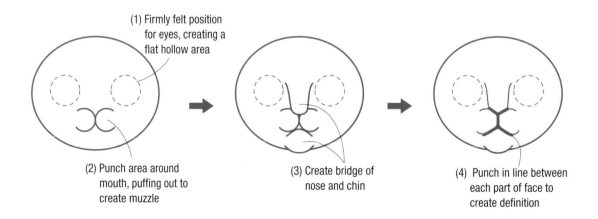

(1) Firmly felt position
for eyes, creating a
flat hollow area

(2) Punch area around
mouth, puffing out to
create muzzle

(3) Create bridge of
nose and chin

(4) Punch in line between
each part of face to
create definition

[HOW TO ATTACH EYES AND WHISKERS]

[HOW TO ATTACH EARS]

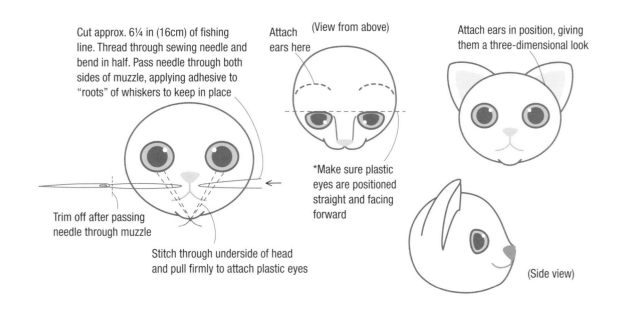

Cut approx. 6¼ in (16cm) of fishing line. Thread through sewing needle and bend in half. Pass needle through both sides of muzzle, applying adhesive to "roots" of whiskers to keep in place

Attach ears here

(View from above)

Attach ears in position, giving them a three-dimensional look

Trim off after passing needle through muzzle

*Make sure plastic eyes are positioned straight and facing forward

Stitch through underside of head and pull firmly to attach plastic eyes

(Side view)

[HOW TO INSERT FLORIST WIRE]

[HOW TO IMPLANT ROVING]

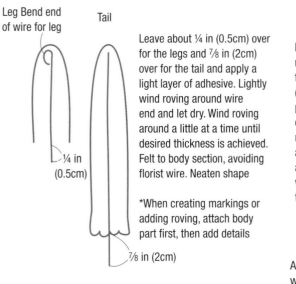

Leg Bend end of wire for leg

Tail

Leave about ¼ in (0.5cm) over for the legs and ⅞ in (2cm) over for the tail and apply a light layer of adhesive. Lightly wind roving around wire end and let dry. Wind roving around a little at a time until desired thickness is achieved. Felt to body section, avoiding florist wire. Neaten shape

*When creating markings or adding roving, attach body part first, then add details

¼ in (0.5cm)

⅞ in (2cm)

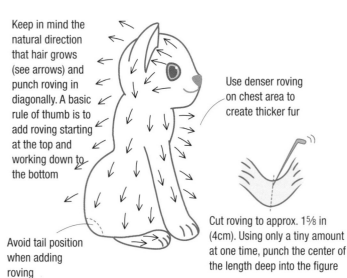

Keep in mind the natural direction that hair grows (see arrows) and punch roving in diagonally. A basic rule of thumb is to add roving starting at the top and working down to the bottom

Use denser roving on chest area to create thicker fur

Avoid tail position when adding roving

Cut roving to approx. 1⅝ in (4cm). Using only a tiny amount at one time, punch the center of the length deep into the figure

🐾 Chinchilla Silver Cat

PAGE 15 **HEIGHT:** 3⅜ in (8.5cm)

🐾 MATERIALS

Roving
  natural blend: white 0.42 oz (12g),
  small amount of pink
  solid: small amount of black
  colored wool: organic wool 0.11 oz (3g),
  blue-faced Leicester 0.07 oz (2g)
Plastic eyes ⅜ in (9mm), crystal blue x 2
Florist wire—6¾ in (17cm)
Fishing line (size 2)—6¼ in (16cm)

1 Create each part, referring to full-size parts diagram as a guide

2 Create face and attach ears

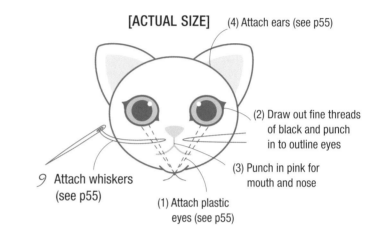

[ACTUAL SIZE]

(4) Attach ears (see p55)

(2) Draw out fine threads of black and punch in to outline eyes

(3) Punch in pink for mouth and nose

9 Attach whiskers (see p55)

(1) Attach plastic eyes (see p55)

6 Add organic wool to head and body (see p55)
*In particular, make sure the fur around the neck and on the chest looks full and luxuriant

3 Slightly tilt head and attach to body

Create expression by adding blue-faced Leicester in around eyebrows and outer edges of eyes and from forehead to back of head

9

5 Use needle to create holes at position for attaching front legs. Bend ends of florist wire, apply adhesive and insert

(Back view)

Add blue-faced Leicester from back of head along back to tail to create markings

7 Add blue-faced Leicester from the tip of the tail, working up and mixing gradually with organic wool to create gradation. (At the underside of tail base, use organic wool only). Attach tail to body as per front legs

Slightly bend tips of paws to create pose

8 Trim wool and neaten into shape
*Trim to shorter length around face and on belly

4 Flatten underside so cat can stand unsupported. Attach hind legs

56

FULL-SIZE PARTS

Use florist wire to create core for front legs and tail (see p55). Use white unless otherwise specified

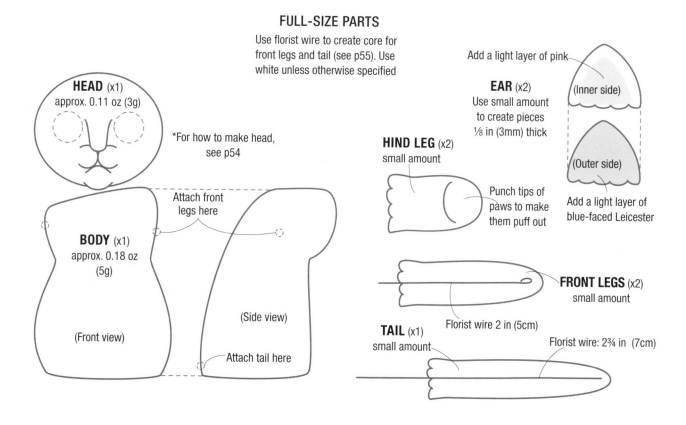

HEAD (x1)
approx. 0.11 oz (3g)

*For how to make head, see p54

BODY (x1)
approx. 0.18 oz (5g)

(Front view)

Attach front legs here

(Side view)

Attach tail here

Add a light layer of pink

EAR (x2)
Use small amount to create pieces ⅛ in (3mm) thick

(Inner side)

(Outer side)

Add a light layer of blue-faced Leicester

HIND LEG (x2)
small amount

Punch tips of paws to make them puff out

FRONT LEGS (x2)
small amount

Florist wire 2 in (5cm)

TAIL (x1)
small amount

Florist wire: 2¾ in (7cm)

❧ Norwegian Forest Cat

PAGE 15   **HEIGHT:** 4 in (10cm)

❧ MATERIALS

Roving
  natural blend: white 0.49 oz (14g), small
  amount each of light brown and pink
  solid: small amount of dark brown
  colored wool: blue-faced Leicester 0.11oz (3g),
  Shetland 0.07 oz (2g)
Plastic eyes ⅜ in (9mm), green x 2
Florist wire—6½ in (16.5cm)
Fishing line (size 2)—12⅝ in (32cm)

1 Create each part, referring to full-size parts diagram as a guide

2 Create face and attach ears

[ACTUAL SIZE]

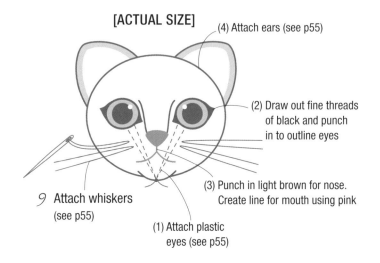

(4) Attach ears (see p55)

(2) Draw out fine threads of black and punch in to outline eyes

(3) Punch in light brown for nose. Create line for mouth using pink

9 Attach whiskers (see p55)

(1) Attach plastic eyes (see p55)

3 Attach head to body

Add roving working from top to bottom

Add roving from center of head, working out to edges

6 Add Shetland to forehead, cheeks, chest, belly and area from ankles to toes. Add blue-faced Leicester around face, at back of head, from sides to center of back, and on hindquarters (see p55)

*Make the chest area particularly full and luxuriant using Shetland

7 Add blue-faced Leicester to tail, starting at tip. Insert florist wire in tail as per front legs and attach to body

When adding roving, leave position for attaching tail free

8 Trim hair that is too long and neaten shape to finish
*Make hair short around face and on belly

5 Use needle to create holes at position for attaching front legs. Bend ends of florist wire, apply adhesive and insert

4 Flatten underside so cat sits upright unsupported. Attach hind legs

FULL-SIZE PARTS

Use florist wire to create core for
front legs and tail (see p55)

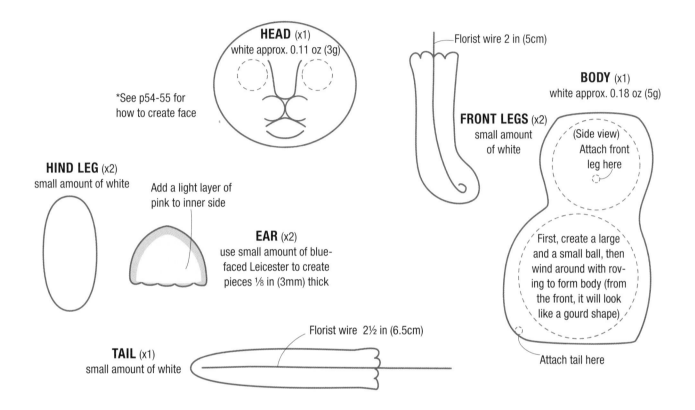

HEAD (x1)
white approx. 0.11 oz (3g)

*See p54-55 for
how to create face

Florist wire 2 in (5cm)

BODY (x1)
white approx. 0.18 oz (5g)

FRONT LEGS (x2)
small amount
of white

(Side view)
Attach front
leg here

HIND LEG (x2)
small amount of white

Add a light layer of
pink to inner side

EAR (x2)
use small amount of blue-
faced Leicester to create
pieces ⅛ in (3mm) thick

First, create a large
and a small ball, then
wind around with rov-
ing to form body (from
the front, it will look
like a gourd shape)

Florist wire 2½ in (6.5cm)

TAIL (x1)
small amount of white

Attach tail here

♣ The Abyssinian

PAGE 16 HEIGHT: 4⅜ in (11cm)

♣ MATERIALS

Roving
  natural blend: white 0.39 oz (11g),
  light brown 0.07 oz (2g);
  small amounts each of dark brown and pink
  mix: small amount of brown
  solid: small amount of dark brown
Plastic eyes ⅜ in (9mm), crystal brown x 2
Florist wire—14¼ in (36cm)
Fishing line (size 2)—6¼ in (16cm)

1 Create each part, referring to full-size parts diagram as a guide

2 Create face and attach ears

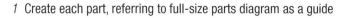

(1) Punch in light brown, leaving areas around nose and mouth and around eyes white

[ACTUAL SIZE]

(7) Attach ears (see p55)

(3) Attach white around eyes to form eyebrows

(6) Add light layer of dark brown to create markings

(4) Punch in brown for nose

8 Attach whiskers (see p55)

(5) Punch in pink for mouth

(2) Attach plastic eyes (see p55)

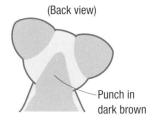

(Back view)

Punch in dark brown

6 Add a light layer of dark brown from back of head along back

3 Tilt head slightly and attach to body

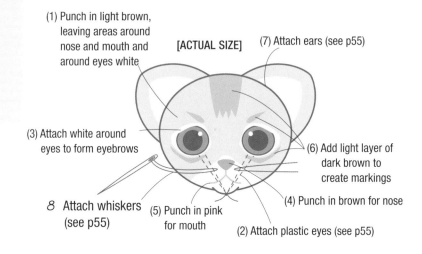

7 Use needle to create hole at position for attaching tail. Bend end of florist wire, apply adhesive and insert. Felt area around base of tail firmly

4 Create claws. Use needle to create holes at position for attaching front legs. Bend ends of florist wire, apply adhesive and insert. Attach front and hind legs, checking balance and felting firmly around joins so cat can stand unsupported

5 Add light brown to shoulders and haunches and punch in

Draw out fine threads of dark brown and punch in

FULL-SIZE PARTS

Use florist wire to create core for front legs and tail (see p55)

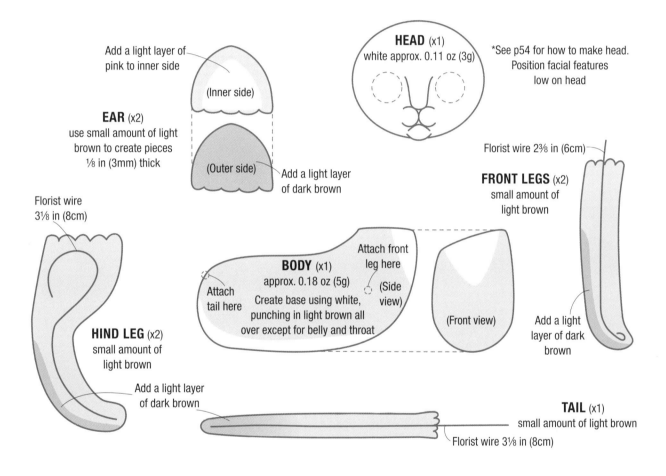

Add a light layer of pink to inner side

(Inner side)

EAR (x2)
use small amount of light brown to create pieces ⅛ in (3mm) thick

(Outer side)

Add a light layer of dark brown

HEAD (x1)
white approx. 0.11 oz (3g)

*See p54 for how to make head.
Position facial features
low on head

Florist wire 2⅜ in (6cm)

FRONT LEGS (x2)
small amount of light brown

Florist wire 3⅛ in (8cm)

BODY (x1)
approx. 0.18 oz (5g)
Create base using white, punching in light brown all over except for belly and throat

Attach front leg here

(Side view)

Attach tail here

(Front view)

Add a light layer of dark brown

HIND LEG (x2)
small amount of light brown

Add a light layer of dark brown

TAIL (x1)
small amount of light brown

Florist wire 3⅛ in (8cm)

❦ The Munchkin

PAGE 17 **HEIGHT:** 3⅜ in (8.5cm)

❦ MATERIALS

Roving
  natural blend: white 0.32 oz (9g),
  small amount of pink
  mix: small amount of yellow beige and brown
  solid: small amount of dark brown
Plastic eyes ⅜ in (9mm), light brown x 2
Florist wire—3 in (7.5cm)
Fishing line (size 2)—6¼ in (16cm)

1 Create each part, referring to full-size parts diagram as a guide

2 Create face and attach ears

[ACTUAL SIZE]

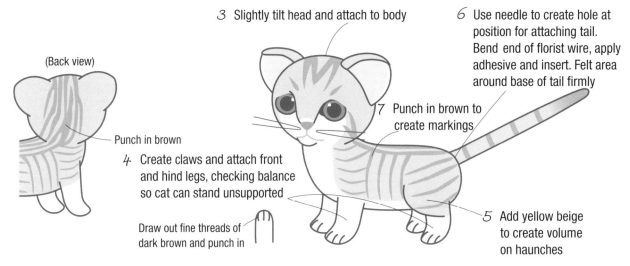

(3) Draw out fine threads of dark brown and punch in to create outline of eyes

(1) Punch in yellow beige, leaving muzzle and tip of nose white

(7) Attach ears (see p55)

(4) Attach yellow beige around eyes to create eyelids

(5) Punch in brown to create markings

(6) Punch in pink for nose and mouth

8 Attach whiskers (see p55)

(2) Attach plastic eyes (see p55)

3 Slightly tilt head and attach to body

6 Use needle to create hole at position for attaching tail. Bend end of florist wire, apply adhesive and insert. Felt area around base of tail firmly

(Back view)

Punch in brown

7 Punch in brown to create markings

4 Create claws and attach front and hind legs, checking balance so cat can stand unsupported

Draw out fine threads of dark brown and punch in

5 Add yellow beige to create volume on haunches

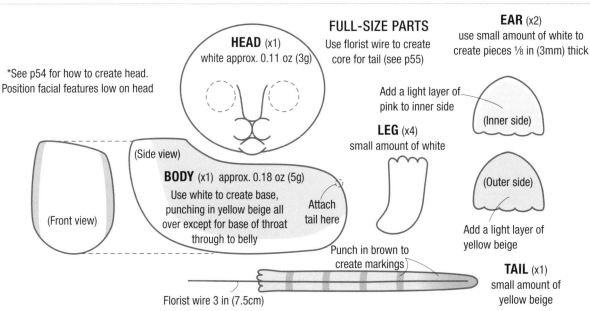

*See p54 for how to create head. Position facial features low on head

FULL-SIZE PARTS

HEAD (x1)
white approx. 0.11 oz (3g)

Use florist wire to create core for tail (see p55)

EAR (x2)
use small amount of white to create pieces ⅛ in (3mm) thick

Add a light layer of pink to inner side

(Inner side)

LEG (x4)
small amount of white

(Outer side)

Add a light layer of yellow beige

(Front view)

(Side view)

BODY (x1) approx. 0.18 oz (5g)
Use white to create base, punching in yellow beige all over except for base of throat through to belly

Attach tail here

Punch in brown to create markings

TAIL (x1)
small amount of yellow beige

Florist wire 3 in (7.5cm)

❧ Little Birds (The Budgerigar, The Java Finch, The Cockatiel)

PAGE 18, 19
LENGTH:
Budgerigar—large 2¾ in (7cm), small 2 in (5 cm)
Cockatiel—large 3 in (7.5cm), small 1¾ in (4.5cm)
Java Finch—1⅞ in (4.8cm)

❧ MATERIALS
BUDGERIGAR (LARGE)
Roving
   solid: pea green 0.25 oz (7g), yellow 0.018 oz
   (0.5g); small amounts each of sky blue
   and cream
   mix: small amount of yellow beige
   natural blend: small amounts each of light
   brown and dark grey
Solid eyes ⅛ in (4mm) x 2

BUDGERIGAR (SMALL)
Roving
   solid: sky blue 0.11 oz (3g); small amounts each
   of cream, bright yellow and blue
   natural blend: grey 0.014 oz (0.4g)
Solid eyes ⅛ in (3mm) x 2

COCKATIEL (LARGE)
Roving
   mix: grey 0.21 oz (6g)
   solid: yellow 0.007 oz (0.2g); small amounts
   each of pale yellow, white, orange (16)
   natural blend: grey 0.053 oz (1.5g);
   small amount of pink
Solid eyes ⅛ in (4mm) x 2

COCKATIEL (SMALL)
Roving
   solid: cream 0.12 oz (3.5g), yellow 0.007 oz
   (0.2g), pale yellow 0.0035 oz (0.1g);
   small amount of orange
   natural blend: small amounts each of beige
   and dark grey
Solid eyes ⅛ in (3mm) x 2

JAVA FINCH
Roving
   solid: black 0.028 oz (0.8g), red 0.007 oz (0.2g)
   natural blend: red brown 0.046 oz (1.3g);
   small amounts each of white and pink
Solid eyes ⅛ in (3mm) x 2

1 Create parts, referring to full-size parts diagrams as a guide.
For Java Finch, attach head to body

〈BUDGERIGAR〉

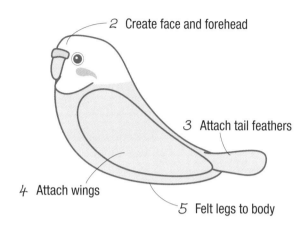

2 Create face and forehead
3 Attach tail feathers
4 Attach wings
5 Felt legs to body

〈COCKATIEL〉

3 Attach crest from bridge of beak to back of head
2 Create face and forehead
4 Attach tail feathers
5 Attach wings
6 Felt legs to body

〈JAVA FINCH〉

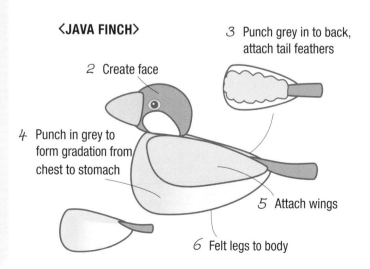

3 Punch grey in to back, attach tail feathers
2 Create face
4 Punch in grey to form gradation from chest to stomach
5 Attach wings
6 Felt legs to body

2 Create face and forehead

[ACTUAL SIZE]

⟨BUDGERIGAR: LARGE⟩

(5) Punch in same color as face to create filled out forehead

(2) Attach bridge of beak. For large: use light brown; for small: use sky blue

(3) Use needle to create eye holes. Apply adhesive to solid eyes and insert into holes. For large size only, work through cream to create outline around eyes

(4) Punch in same color as face to create cheeks. Create markings in sky blue (large size) or blue (small size)

(1) Attach beak

⟨COCKATIEL: LARGE⟩

(4) Punch in same color as face to create filled out forehead

(2) Use needle to create eye holes. Apply adhesive to solid eyes and insert into holes. Punch in white (for large size) and beige (for small size) to create outline around eyes

(3) For both large and small sizes, punch in yellow for cheeks, punching orange in after that

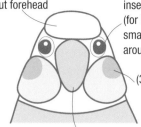

(1) Attach beak

⟨BUDGERIGAR: SMALL⟩

⟨JAVA FINCH⟩

(3) Punch in white for cheeks

(2) Use needle to create eye holes. Apply adhesive to solid eyes and insert into holes. Punch in red to create outline around eyes

(1) Attach beak

⟨COCKATIEL: SMALL⟩

[HOW TO CREATE FEET]

Draw out fine threads in specified color and punch in

[ACTUAL SIZE]

⟨BUDGERIGAR⟩

Large: dark grey   Small: grey

⟨COCKATIEL⟩

Large: pink   Small: dark grey

⟨JAVA FINCH⟩

Pink

FULL-SIZE PARTS

BEAK (x1)
small amount of red

HEAD (x1)
black approx. 0.025 oz (0.7g)

Tilt head upwards and attach to body

BODY (x1)
red brown approx. 0.046 oz (1.3g)

WING (x2)
small amount of grey
Create piece ⅟₁₆ in (2mm) thick

⟨JAVA FINCH⟩

TAIL FEATHERS (x1)
small amount of black. Create pieces ⅛ in (4mm) thick

*For full-size parts for [Budgerigar: large, small] and Cockatiel (large and small) are on next page

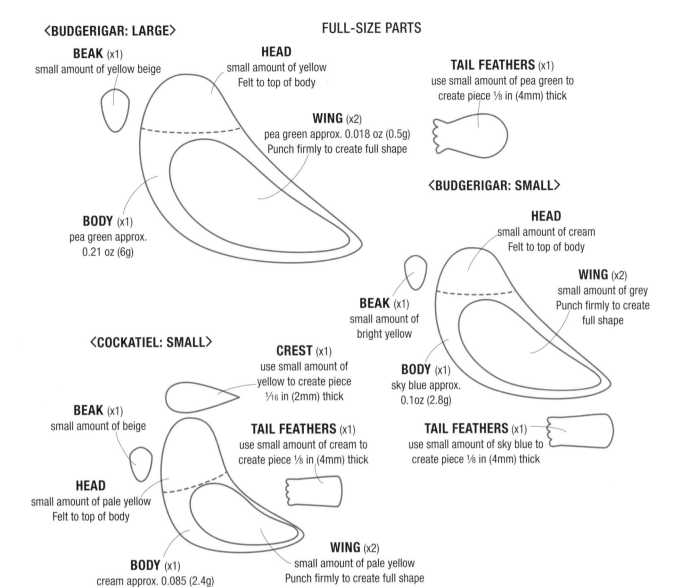

<BUDGERIGAR: LARGE>

BEAK (x1)
small amount of yellow beige

HEAD
small amount of yellow
Felt to top of body

WING (x2)
pea green approx. 0.018 oz (0.5g)
Punch firmly to create full shape

BODY (x1)
pea green approx.
0.21 oz (6g)

TAIL FEATHERS (x1)
use small amount of pea green to
create piece ⅛ in (4mm) thick

<BUDGERIGAR: SMALL>

HEAD
small amount of cream
Felt to top of body

WING (x2)
small amount of grey
Punch firmly to create
full shape

BEAK (x1)
small amount of
bright yellow

BODY (x1)
sky blue approx.
0.1oz (2.8g)

TAIL FEATHERS (x1)
use small amount of sky blue to
create piece ⅛ in (4mm) thick

<COCKATIEL: SMALL>

CREST (x1)
use small amount of
yellow to create piece
1/16 in (2mm) thick

BEAK (x1)
small amount of beige

TAIL FEATHERS (x1)
use small amount of cream to
create piece ⅛ in (4mm) thick

HEAD
small amount of pale yellow
Felt to top of body

BODY (x1)
cream approx. 0.085 (2.4g)

WING (x2)
small amount of pale yellow
Punch firmly to create full shape

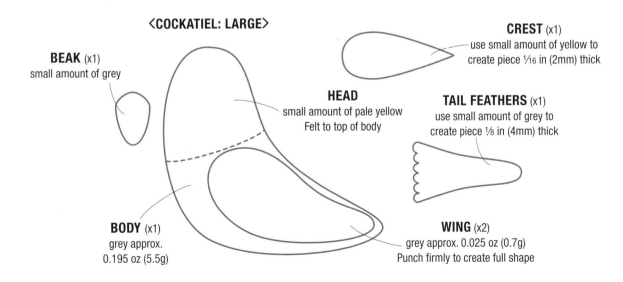

<COCKATIEL: LARGE>

CREST (x1)
use small amount of yellow to
create piece 1/16 in (2mm) thick

BEAK (x1)
small amount of grey

HEAD
small amount of pale yellow
Felt to top of body

TAIL FEATHERS (x1)
use small amount of grey to
create piece ⅛ in (4mm) thick

BODY (x1)
grey approx.
0.195 oz (5.5g)

WING (x2)
grey approx. 0.025 oz (0.7g)
Punch firmly to create full shape

♣ Chipmunks (Large)

LENGTH: 3½ in (9cm)

♣ MATERIALS

Roving

   mix: beige 0.17 oz (4.9g), khaki 0.039 oz (1.1g)
   solid: small amounts each of dark brown and
   black
   natural blend: small amounts each of white,
   dark brown, dark grey
Solid eyes ⅛ in (3mm) x 2

FULL-SIZE PARTS

EAR (x2)
use small amount of khaki to
create pieces 1⁄16 in (2mm) thick

(Front view) (Side view)

HEAD (x1)
beige approx. 0.028 oz (0.8g)

FRONT LEGS (x2)
small amount of beige

BODY (x1)
beige approx.
0.1 oz (2.8g)

HIND LEG (x2)
small amount of beige

(View from above)

TAIL (x1)
khaki approx.
0.032 oz (0.9g)

Add 3 lines of dark grey

(Side view)

Punch firmly in a bent position

1 Create each part, referring to full-size
   parts diagram as a guide

2 Connect body and head, adding beige
   to neck to create a smooth join

(Head)

[ACTUAL SIZE]

5

3 Attach front legs

4 Punch in lines for
   haunches, fluffing out
   before attaching hind legs

6

7

8 Attach tail

5 Create face and attach ears

(4) Attach ears

(3) Punch in khaki from tip of nose to
    base of tail to create markings

(1) Use needle to create eye holes.
    Apply adhesive to eyes and
    insert into holes, then use black
    to create eye outline

(6) Punch in white and dark
    brown to create facial
    markings

(2) Punch in beige under eyes,
    puffing out to create cheeks

(5) Punch in dark brown
    for nose and dark brown
    for mouth

6 Punch in white for belly

[ACTUAL SIZE]

7 Create markings on back

Khaki

Punch in white
in two places

Punch in 5 lines
of dark grey

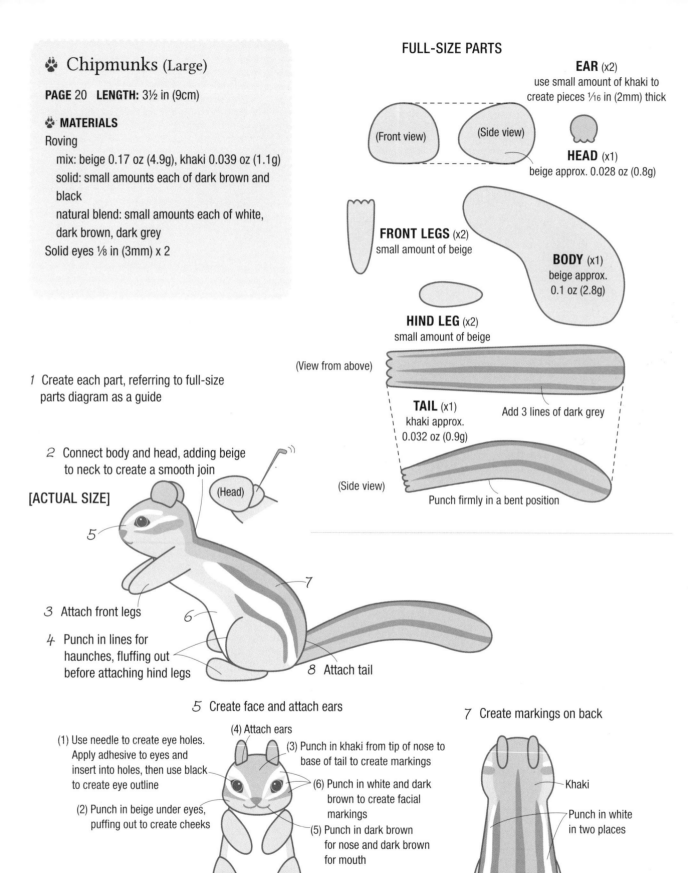

♣ Chipmunks (Small)

PAGE 20   **HEIGHT:** 1¼ in (3cm)

♣ MATERIALS

Roving
  natural blend: light brown 0.014 oz (0.4g);
  small amounts each of red brown 0.011 oz
  (0.3g) and dark grey
  solid: small amount of white
Solid eyes ⅛ in (3mm) x 2

FULL-SIZE PARTS

HEAD (x1)
light brown approx. 0.0035 oz (0.1g)

(Front view)   (Side view)

EAR (x2)
use small amount of light brown to create pieces ⅟₁₆ in (2mm) thick

FRONT LEGS (x2)
small amount of light brown

BODY (x1)
light brown approx. 0.007 oz (0.2g)

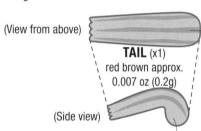

HIND LEG (x2)
small amount of light brown

(View from above)

Add 3 lines of dark grey

TAIL (x1)
red brown approx. 0.007 oz (0.2g)

(Side view)

Felt firmly in a bent position

---

1 Create each part, referring to full-size parts diagram as a guide

2 Attach head to body

3

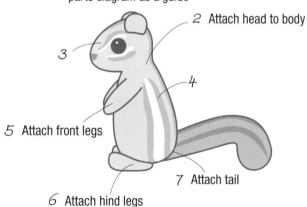

4

5 Attach front legs

7 Attach tail

6 Attach hind legs

[ACTUAL SIZE]

3 Create face and attach ears

(3) Punch in red brown from forehead to base of tail to create markings

(1) Use needle to create eye holes. Apply adhesive to eyes and insert into holes, then use black to create eye outline

(2) Attach ears

(4) Punch in red brown for nose

(5) Punch in white and red brown to create facial markings

4 Create markings on back

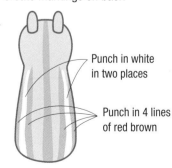

Punch in white in two places

Punch in 4 lines of red brown

❦ Tiny Birds (Red-breasted Parakeet, White Java Finch, Peach-faced Lovebird)

PAGE 21

LENGTH:

Red-breasted parakeet: 1 in (2.5cm)

White Java Finch: ¾ in (1.8cm)

Peach-faced Lovebird: ⅞ in (2.2cm)

❦ MATERIALS

(RED-BREASTED PARAKEET)

Roving

    natural blend: moss green 0.011 oz (0.3g); small amounts each of pink and dark grey

    solid: small amounts each of dark grey, white, pale green, orange

No. 25 embroidery thread (black)

(WHITE JAVA FINCH)

Roving

    natural blend: white 0.011 oz (0.3g); small amount of pink

    solid: small amount of red

No. 25 embroidery thread (black)

(PEACH-FACED LOVEBIRD)

Roving

    solid: pea green 0.011 oz (0.3g), orange green 0.007 oz (0.2g); small amounts each of orange, sky blue, cream

    natural blend: small amount of dark grey

No. 25 embroidery thread (black)

FULL-SIZE PARTS

<RED-BREASTED PARAKEET>

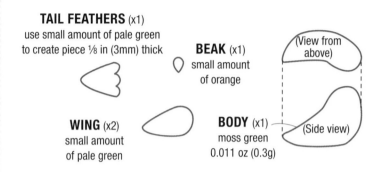

TAIL FEATHERS (x1)
use small amount of pale green
to create piece ⅛ in (3mm) thick

BEAK (x1)
small amount
of orange

(View from above)

WING (x2)
small amount
of pale green

BODY (x1)
moss green
0.011 oz (0.3g)

(Side view)

<WHITE JAVA FINCH>

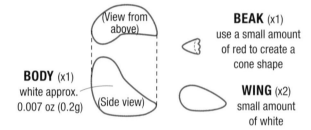

(View from above)

BEAK (x1)
use a small amount
of red to create a
cone shape

BODY (x1)
white approx.
0.007 oz (0.2g)

(Side view)

WING (x2)
small amount
of white

<PEACH-FACED LOVEBIRD>

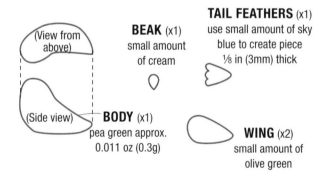

BEAK (x1)
small amount
of cream

TAIL FEATHERS (x1)
use small amount of sky
blue to create piece
⅛ in (3mm) thick

(View from above)

(Side view)

BODY (x1)
pea green approx.
0.011 oz (0.3g)

WING (x2)
small amount of
olive green

1 Create each part, referring to full-size parts diagram as a guide

<RED-BREASTED PARAKEET: ACTUAL SIZE>

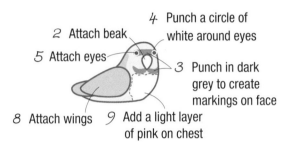

4 Punch a circle of white around eyes

2 Attach beak

5 Attach eyes

3 Punch in dark grey to create markings on face

8 Attach wings

9 Add a light layer of pink on chest

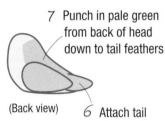

7 Punch in pale green from back of head down to tail feathers

(Back view)

6 Attach tail feathers

10 Draw out fine threads of dark grey and punch in to create feet

(View from below)

<WHITE JAVA FINCH: ACTUAL SIZE>

3 Punch a circle of red around eyes

2 Attach beak

4 Attach eyes

5 Attach wings

(Back view)

6 Draw out fine threads of pink and punch in to create feet

(View from below)

[HOW TO ATTACH EYES: SAME FOR ALL BIRDS]

Thread No. 25 embroidery thread on to needle and stitch through from back of head to eye position, fastening with a knot to create eye

<PEACH-FACED LOVEBIRD: ACTUAL SIZE>

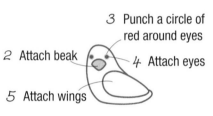

2 Punch in orange on face

4 Attach eyes

5 Attach tail feathers

3 Attach beak

6 Attach wings

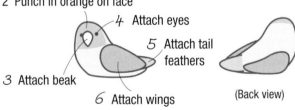

(Back view)

6 Draw out fine threads of dark grey and punch in to create feet

(View from below)

Once the eyes have been created, fasten knot at back of head and trim, concealing knot under a layer of roving the same color as the head

(View from above)

♣ Ferrets (Large)

PAGE 22 **LENGTH:** 6 in (15cm)

♣ MATERIALS

Roving
 natural blend: white 0.21 oz (6g), dark brown
 0.07 oz (2g); small amount of pink
 mix: small amount of beige
Solid eyes ¼ in (6mm) x 2

1 Create parts, referring to full-size parts diagram as a guide

2 Create face and attach ears

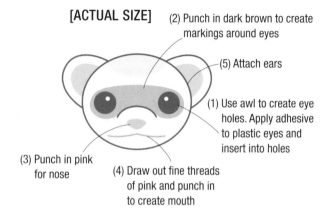

[ACTUAL SIZE]

(2) Punch in dark brown to create markings around eyes

(5) Attach ears

(1) Use awl to create eye holes. Apply adhesive to plastic eyes and insert into holes

(3) Punch in pink for nose

(4) Draw out fine threads of pink and punch in to create mouth

3 Tilt head slightly to the right and attach to head

7 Punch in a fine layer of beige over entire back from crown to base of tail

6 Attach tail

4 Flatten underside so rear end doesn't stick up. Attach hind legs

5 Attach front legs, checking balance to ensure hind quarters and hind legs don't stick up

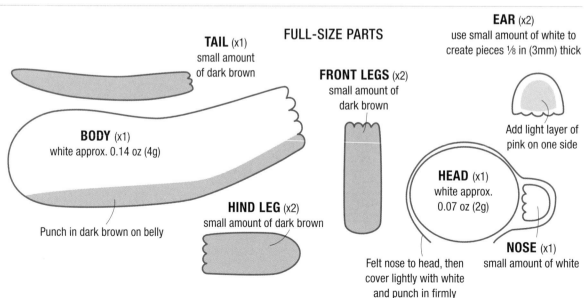

FULL-SIZE PARTS

TAIL (x1)
small amount of dark brown

FRONT LEGS (x2)
small amount of dark brown

EAR (x2)
use small amount of white to create pieces ⅛ in (3mm) thick

Add light layer of pink on one side

BODY (x1)
white approx. 0.14 oz (4g)

Punch in dark brown on belly

HEAD (x1)
white approx. 0.07 oz (2g)

HIND LEG (x2)
small amount of dark brown

Felt nose to head, then cover lightly with white and punch in firmly

NOSE (x1)
small amount of white

🐾 Ferrets (Small)

PAGE 22 **HEIGHT:** 2 in (5cm)

🐾 MATERIALS

Roving
  natural blend: beige 0.06 oz (1.7g);
  small amount of pink
  mix: khaki 0.014 oz (0.4g)
Solid eyes ⅛ in (3mm) x 2

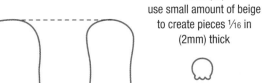

FULL-SIZE PARTS

EAR (x2)
use small amount of beige
to create pieces ¹⁄₁₆ in
(2mm) thick

FRONT LEGS (x2)
small amount of khaki

(Side view) (Front view)

BODY (x1)
beige approx. 0.056 oz (1.6g)

HIND LEG (x2)
small amount of khaki

TAIL (x1)
khaki approx. 0.0035 oz (0.1g)

---

1 Create parts, referring to full-size parts diagram as a guide

2 Create face and attach ears

[ACTUAL SIZE]

(2) Use needle to create hole.
  Apply adhesive to solid
  eye and insert into hole

(1) Attach ears

(3) Punch in khaki to
  create markings
  around eyes

(4) Punch in pink
  for nose

(5) Draw out fine threads
  of khaki and punch in
  to create mouth

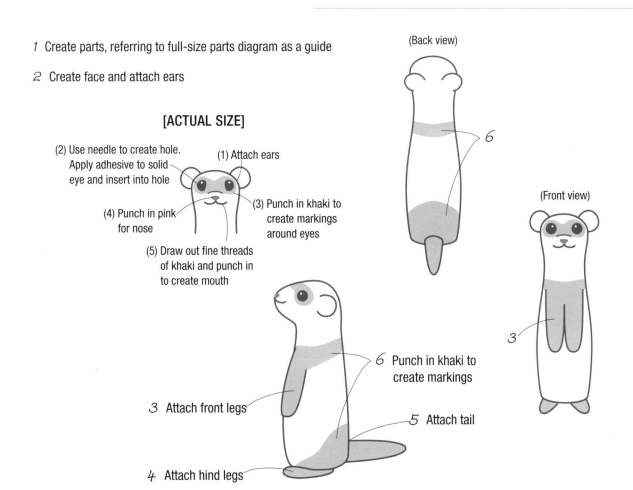

(Back view)

6

(Front view)

3

6 Punch in khaki to
  create markings

3 Attach front legs

5 Attach tail

4 Attach hind legs

❧ Hamsters

PAGE 23   **STANDING FIGURE: HEIGHT:** 2½ in (6.5cm);
             PRONE FIGURE: LENGTH: 2½ in (6.5cm)

❧ MATERIALS

Roving
   mix: beige 0.165 oz (4.7g)
   natural blend: white 0.018 oz (0.5g);
   small amount of dark brown
Solid eyes ⅛ in (4mm) x 2

[FOR SUNFLOWER SEED]
Roving
   solid: small amounts each of beige and black

1   Create parts, referring to full-size parts diagram as a guide

2   Attach ears to head and create face

[ACTUAL SIZE]
*Instructions are the same for each figure unless otherwise specified

[STANDING FIGURE]

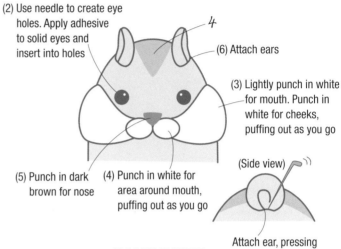

(2) Use needle to create eye holes. Apply adhesive to solid eyes and insert into holes

4

(6) Attach ears

(3) Lightly punch in white for mouth. Punch in white for cheeks, puffing out as you go

(5) Punch in dark brown for nose

(4) Punch in white for area around mouth, puffing out as you go

(Side view)

Attach ear, pressing inwards at center

[PRONE FIGURE]

4

3   Attach front and hind legs and tail to body

[PRONE FIGURE]

[ACTUAL SIZE]

(Back view)

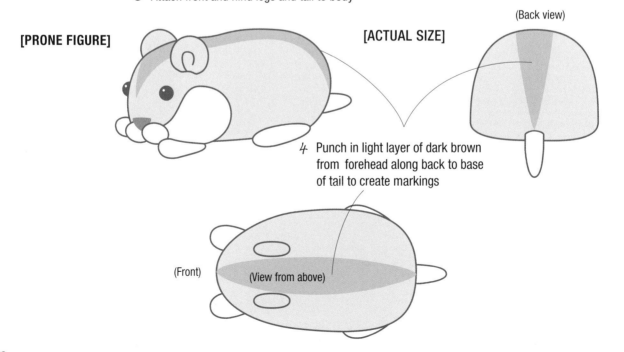

4   Punch in light layer of dark brown from forehead along back to base of tail to create markings

(Front)

(View from above)

3 Attach hind legs and tail to body

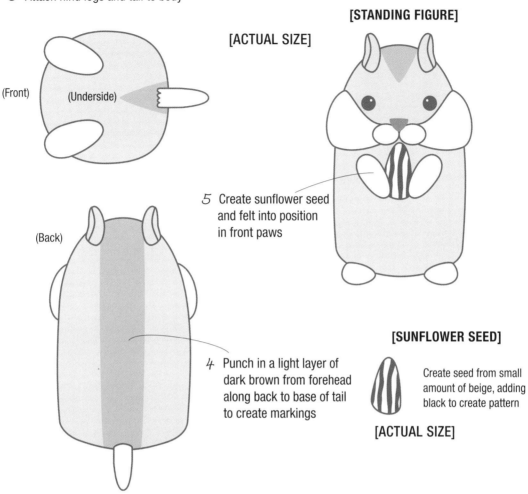

[STANDING FIGURE]

[ACTUAL SIZE]

(Front)

(Underside)

(Back)

5 Create sunflower seed and felt into position in front paws

4 Punch in a light layer of dark brown from forehead along back to base of tail to create markings

[SUNFLOWER SEED]

Create seed from small amount of beige, adding black to create pattern

[ACTUAL SIZE]

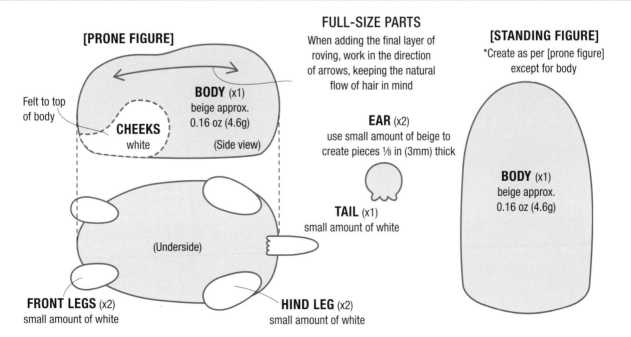

[PRONE FIGURE]

Felt to top of body

CHEEKS white

BODY (x1) beige approx. 0.16 oz (4.6g)

(Side view)

(Underside)

FRONT LEGS (x2) small amount of white

HIND LEG (x2) small amount of white

FULL-SIZE PARTS

When adding the final layer of roving, work in the direction of arrows, keeping the natural flow of hair in mind

EAR (x2) use small amount of beige to create pieces ⅛ in (3mm) thick

TAIL (x1) small amount of white

[STANDING FIGURE]

*Create as per [prone figure] except for body

BODY (x1) beige approx. 0.16 oz (4.6g)

73

🐾 Three Kinds of Rabbit

PAGE 24 **HEIGHT:** 3 in (7.5cm)

🐾 MATERIALS

(FOR WHITE: A)

Roving

    solid: white 0.21 oz (6g); small amount of dark brown

    natural blend: small amount of pink

    mix: small amount of pea green

Glass eyes ⅛ in (4mm) x 2

Fishing line (size 2)—4¾ in (12cm)

Felt (grey): 1⅝ in x 1¼ in (4cm x 3cm) x 4 sheets;
         1¼ in x 1¼ in (3cm x 3cm) x 1 sheet

Cotton thread (white)

(FOR BROWN: B)

Roving

    solid: white 0.21 oz (6g); small amount of dark brown

    natural blend: light brown 0.21 oz (6g);

    small amount of pink

    mix: small amount of pea green

Glass eyes ⅛ in (4mm) x 2

Fishing line (size 2)—4¾ in (12cm)

Felt (grey): 1⅝ in x 1¼ in (4cm x 3cm) x 4 sheets;
         1¼ in x 1¼ in (3cm x 3cm) x 1 sheet

Cotton thread (white)

(WHITE & GREY: C)

Roving

    solid: white 0.21 oz (6g); small amount of dark brown

    natural blend: grey; small amount of pink

    mix: small amount of pea green

Glass eyes ⅛ in (4mm) x 2

Fishing line (size 2)—4¾ in (12cm)

Felt (grey): 1⅝ in x 1¼ in (4cm x 3cm) x 4 sheets;
         1¼ in x 1¼ in (3cm x 3cm) x 1 sheet

Cotton thread (white)

FULL-SIZE PARTS

HEAD (x1)
approx. 0.07 oz (2g)
A: white;
B: light brown;
C: white

EAR (x2)
use small amounts of
A: white;
B: light brown;
C: grey
to create pieces ⅛ in (3mm) thick

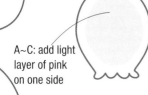

A~C: add light
layer of pink
on one side

BODY (x1)
approx. 0.12 oz (3.5g) of
A: white;
B: light brown;
C: white

FRONT LEGS (x2)
small amount of
A: white;
B: light brown;
C: white

LEAF (x1)
Use small amount of pea
green to create piece
1/16 in (2mm) thick for A~C

FLOWER (x1)
Use small amount of
A: pink;
B: white;
C: pink
to create piece 1/16 in
(2mm) thick

1 Create parts, referring to full-size parts diagram as a guide

2 Create box

Punch in flower and leaf
to one side of 1⅝ in x 1¼
(4cm x 3cm)

Use blanket stitch to assemble box

[BLANKET STITCH]

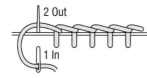

2 Out

1 In

Layer two pieces of felt and stitch using cotton thread

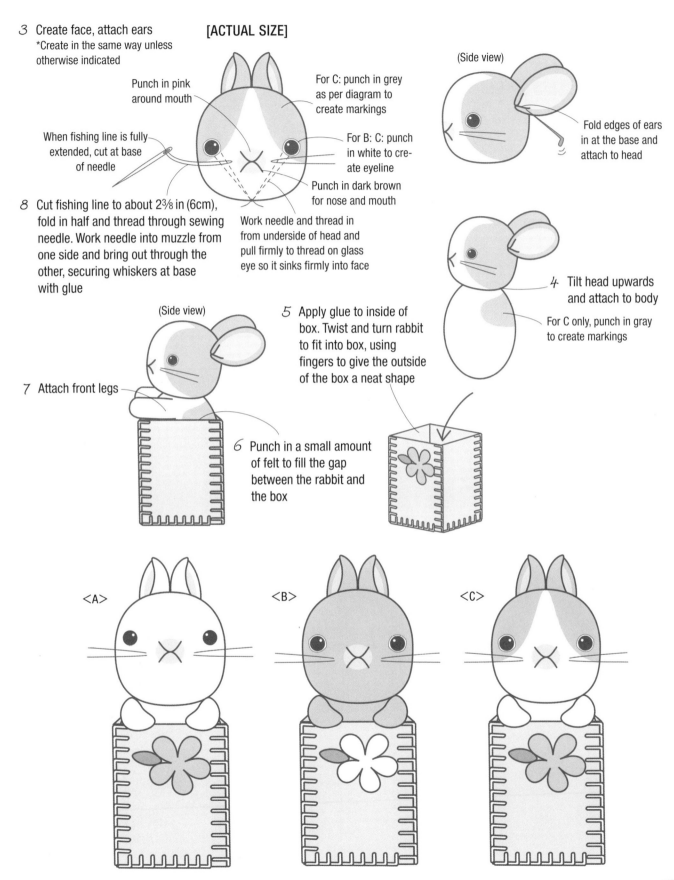

3 Create face, attach ears
*Create in the same way unless otherwise indicated

[ACTUAL SIZE]

Punch in pink around mouth

For C: punch in grey as per diagram to create markings

When fishing line is fully extended, cut at base of needle

For B: C: punch in white to create eyeline

Punch in dark brown for nose and mouth

8 Cut fishing line to about 2⅜ in (6cm), fold in half and thread through sewing needle. Work needle into muzzle from one side and bring out through the other, securing whiskers at base with glue

Work needle and thread in from underside of head and pull firmly to thread on glass eye so it sinks firmly into face

(Side view)

Fold edges of ears in at the base and attach to head

4 Tilt head upwards and attach to body

For C only, punch in gray to create markings

(Side view)

5 Apply glue to inside of box. Twist and turn rabbit to fit into box, using fingers to give the outside of the box a neat shape

7 Attach front legs

6 Punch in a small amount of felt to fill the gap between the rabbit and the box

<A>

<B>

<C>

♣ Phone Strap Decorations: Miniature Shiba

PAGE 25   **HEIGHT:** 1¾ in (4.5cm)

♣ MATERIALS

Felting wool
  natural blend: light brown 0.11 oz (3g), white 0.007 oz (0.2g)
  solid: small amount of black
Solid eyes ⅛ in (3mm) x 2
Fishing line (size 2)—4¾ in (12cm)
Felt (grey): 1⅝ in x 1¼ in (4cm x 3cm) x 4 sheets;
           1¼ in x 1¼ in (3cm x 3cm) x 1 sheet
Cotton thread (white)
Eye pin x 1, strap x 1

1 Create parts, referring to full-size parts diagram as a guide

2 Create face and attach ears

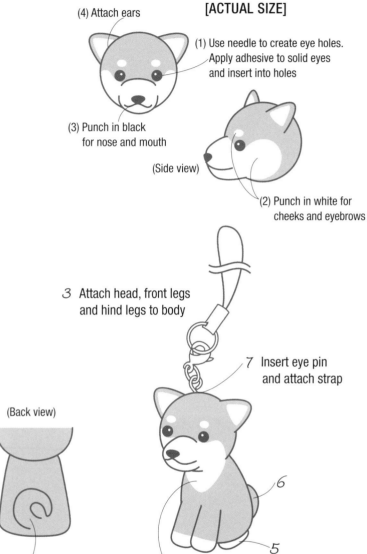

[ACTUAL SIZE]

(4) Attach ears

(1) Use needle to create eye holes. Apply adhesive to solid eyes and insert into holes

(3) Punch in black for nose and mouth

(Side view)

(2) Punch in white for cheeks and eyebrows

3 Attach head, front legs and hind legs to body

7 Insert eye pin and attach strap

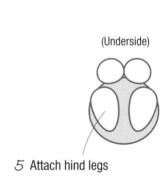

(Underside)

5 Attach hind legs

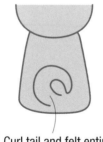

(Back view)

6 Curl tail and felt entire tail snugly to body

4 Add light brown to chest to create volume. Punch in white to create markings

6

5

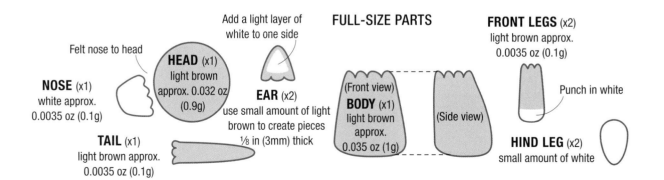

Felt nose to head

NOSE (x1)
white approx.
0.0035 oz (0.1g)

HEAD (x1)
light brown approx. 0.032 oz (0.9g)

Add a light layer of white to one side

EAR (x2)
use small amount of light brown to create pieces ⅛ in (3mm) thick

TAIL (x1)
light brown approx.
0.0035 oz (0.1g)

FULL-SIZE PARTS

(Front view)
BODY (x1)
light brown approx.
0.035 oz (1g)

(Side view)

FRONT LEGS (x2)
light brown approx.
0.0035 oz (0.1g)

Punch in white

HIND LEG (x2)
small amount of white

🐾 Phone Strap Decorations: Miniature Hokkaido Dog

PAGE 25 **HEIGHT:** 2 in (5cm)

🐾 MATERIALS
Roving
  natural blend: white 0.14 oz (4g)
  solid: blue 0.011 oz (0.3g); small amounts
  each of black and cream
Solid eyes ⅛ in (3mm) x 2
Eye pin x 1, strap x 1

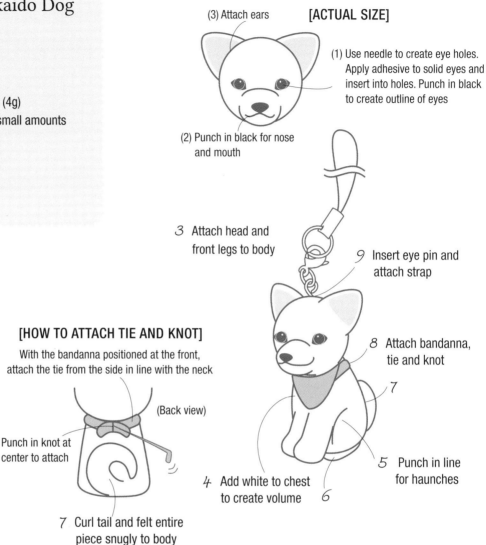

1 Create parts, referring to full-size parts diagram as a guide

2 Create face and attach ears

(3) Attach ears

[ACTUAL SIZE]

(1) Use needle to create eye holes.
   Apply adhesive to solid eyes and
   insert into holes. Punch in black
   to create outline of eyes

(2) Punch in black for nose
   and mouth

3 Attach head and
   front legs to body

9 Insert eye pin and
   attach strap

8 Attach bandanna,
   tie and knot

7

5 Punch in line
   for haunches

6

4 Add white to chest
   to create volume

[HOW TO ATTACH TIE AND KNOT]

With the bandanna positioned at the front,
attach the tie from the side in line with the neck

(Back view)

Punch in knot at
center to attach

(Underside)

6 Attach hind legs

7 Curl tail and felt entire
   piece snugly to body

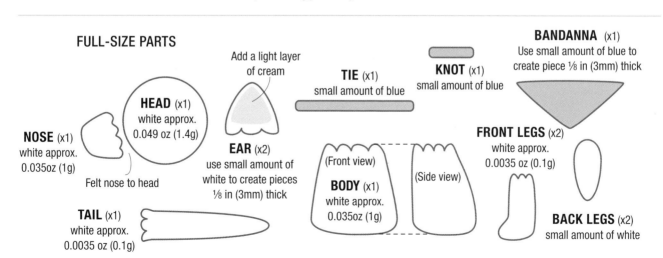

FULL-SIZE PARTS

Add a light layer
of cream

TIE (x1)
small amount of blue

KNOT (x1)
small amount of blue

BANDANNA (x1)
Use small amount of blue to
create piece ⅛ in (3mm) thick

HEAD (x1)
white approx.
0.049 oz (1.4g)

NOSE (x1)
white approx.
0.035oz (1g)

EAR (x2)
use small amount of
white to create pieces
⅛ in (3mm) thick

Felt nose to head

FRONT LEGS (x2)
white approx.
0.0035 oz (0.1g)

(Front view)

BODY (x1)
white approx.
0.035oz (1g)

(Side view)

BACK LEGS (x2)
small amount of white

TAIL (x1)
white approx.
0.0035 oz (0.1g)

♣ Phone Strap Decorations:
Miniature Schnauzer
Miniature Dachshund

PAGE 25 **HEIGHT:** 3 in (7.5cm)

♣ MATERIALS

(MINIATURE DACHSHUND)

Roving
  solid: black 0.11 oz (3g); small amount of white
  natural blend: small amount of light brown
Wool batting—0.18 oz (5g)
Solid eyes ⅛ in (3mm) x 2
Eye pin x 1, strap x 1

(MINIATURE SCHNAUZER)

Roving
  natural blend: dark grey 0.07 oz (2g)
  solid: small amounts each of black and white
Wool batting—0.18 oz (5g)
Solid eyes ⅛ in (3mm) x 2
Eye pin x 1, strap x 1

1 Create parts, referring to full-size parts diagram as a guide

2 Create face and attach ears

⟨MINIATURE DACHSHUND⟩

[ACTUAL SIZE]

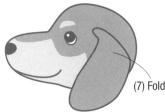

(3) Punch in black all over except for muzzle

(4) Punch in light brown for eyebrows

(2) Punch in light brown for muzzle

(1) Use needle to create eye holes. Apply adhesive to solid eyes and insert into holes

(6) Punch in black for nose and mouth

(5) Punch in white under eyes to give the appearance of upturned eyes. Punch in black line around eyes

(7) Fold over ears and attach

⟨MINIATURE SCHNAUZER⟩

[ACTUAL SIZE]

(3) Punch in dark grey all over except muzzle

(4) Create firmly felted eyebrows using white and felt to head

(7) Fold over ears and attach

(2) Punch in white for muzzle

(1) Use needle to create eye holes. Apply adhesive to solid eyes and insert into holes

(6) Punch in black for nose and mouth

(5) Punch in white under eyes to give the appearance of upturned eyes. Punch in black line around eyes

⟨MINIATURE DACHSHUND⟩

4 Attach head, front legs and hind legs to body. Add wool batting to joins and felt together

5 Add layer of black all over body and punch in, creating markings using light brown

3 Create claws and paw pads
*For front legs, create claw lines on upper side only. For hind legs, create claw lines and paw pads

Draw out fine threads of black and punch in

Black

(Upper side) (Underside)

Tilt head slightly upwards and attach to body

7 Insert eye pin and attach strap

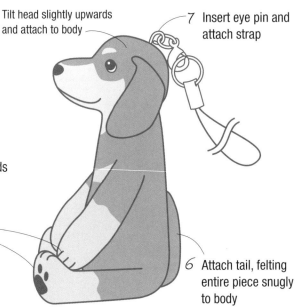

6 Attach tail, felting entire piece snugly to body

⟨MINIATURE SCHNAUZER⟩

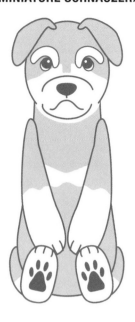

*Refer to instructions for Miniature Dachshund unless otherwise specified

5 Add layer of dark grey over entire body and punch in, using white to create markings

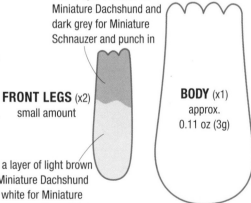

7

3

6 Attach tail

⟨MINIATURE DACHSHUND⟩

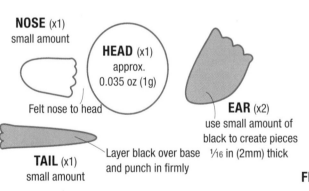

NOSE (x1)
small amount

Felt nose to head

HEAD (x1)
approx.
0.035 oz (1g)

EAR (x2)
use small amount of black to create pieces ¹⁄₁₆ in (2mm) thick

TAIL (x1)
small amount

Layer black over base and punch in firmly

⟨MINIATURE SCHNAUZER⟩

NOSE (x1)
small amount

HEAD (x1)
approx.
0.035 oz (1g)

Felt nose to head

TAIL (x1)
small amount

Layer dark grey over base and punch in firmly

EAR (x2)
use small amount of dark grey to create pieces ¹⁄₁₆ in (2mm) thick

---

FULL-SIZE PARTS

Use wool batting to create base except for ears
*Instructions are the same for both dogs unless otherwise specified

Add a layer of black for Miniature Dachshund and dark grey for Miniature Schnauzer and punch in

FRONT LEGS (x2)
small amount

Add a layer of light brown for Miniature Dachshund and white for Miniature Schnauzer and punch in

BODY (x1)
approx.
0.11 oz (3g)

Add a layer of black for Miniature Dachshund and dark grey for Miniature Schnauzer and punch in

HIND LEG (x2)
small amount

Add a layer of light brown for Miniature Dachshund and white for Miniature Schnauzer and punch in

Published in 2015 by Tuttle Publishing, an imprint of Periplus Editions (HK) Ltd.

www.tuttlepublishing.com

ISBN 978-4-8053-1358-9

Japanese original title: 羊毛フェルトで作る動物絵本
Youmou Felt de Tsukuru Doubutsuehon
© Gakken Publishing 2010
First published in Japan 2010 by Gakken Publishing Co., Ltd., Tokyo
English translation arranged with GAKKEN PUBLISHING CO., LTD.
Through Japan UNI Agency, Inc.,Tokyo

English Translation © 2015 Periplus Editions (HK) Ltd.
Translated from Japanese by Leeyong Soo
All rights reserved.

Original Japanese edition:
Design: s@chi, Sareee, Campanella, Satomi Fujita
Photography: Miwa Kumon
Step-by-step photography: Ayumi Nakatsuji
Book design: Mihoko Amano, Nanako Futoda
Editors: Kyoko Nishida, Tomoko Kodera (Gakken Publishing); Shuko Sato (Little Bird)

Distributed by
North America, Latin America & Europe
Tuttle Publishing
364 Innovation Drive, North Clarendon, VT 05759-9436 U.S.A.
Tel: 1 (802) 773-8930; Fax: 1 (802) 773-6993
info@tuttlepublishing.com
www.tuttlepublishing.com

Japan
Tuttle Publishing
Yaekari Building, 3rd Floor, 5-4-12 Osaki, Shinagawa-ku, Tokyo 141 0032
Tel: (81) 3 5437-0171; Fax: (81) 3 5437-0755
sales@tuttle.co.jp
www.tuttle.co.jp

Asia Pacific
Berkeley Books Pte. Ltd.
61 Tai Seng Avenue #02-12, Singapore 534167
Tel: (65) 6280-1330; Fax: (65) 6280-6290
inquiries@periplus.com.sg
www.periplus.com

Printed in China   1601RR
18 17 16   6 5 4 3 2

TUTTLE PUBLISHING® is a registered trademark of Tuttle Publishing,
a division of Periplus Editions (HK) Ltd.

About Tuttle
"Books to Span the East and West"

Our core mission at Tuttle Publishing is to create
books which bring people together one page at a time.
Tuttle was founded in 1832 in the small New England
town of Rutland, Vermont (USA). Our fundamental
values remain as strong today as they were then—to
publish best-in-class books informing the English-
speaking world about the countries and peoples of
Asia. The world has become a smaller place today and
Asia's economic, cultural and political influence has
expanded, yet the need for meaningful dialogue and
information about this diverse region has never been
greater. Since 1948, Tuttle has been a leader in
publishing books on the cultures, arts, cuisines,
languages and literatures of Asia. Our authors and
photographers have won numerous awards and Tuttle
has published thousands of books on subjects ranging
from martial arts to paper crafts. We welcome you to
explore the wealth of information available on Asia at
www.tuttlepublishing.com.